DR. MAHESH PATIL'S
REVERSE DIABETES
AND
RECLAIM YOUR LIFE

The Science Backed Plan to Reset Insulin and Heal Naturally

Contents

Prologue 1

Introduction 3

1 What Is Diabetes – And Why You Can Reverse It 7

2 What If Everything You Knew About Diabetes Was Wrong? 17

3 How Diabetes Can Actually Be Reversed 23

4 Eat to Heal–The Diabetes Reversal Diet 27

5 Move to Heal–How Exercise Reverses Diabetes 31

6 Stress & Sleep—The Hidden Keys to Healing 35

7 Habits That Heal–The Secret to Long-Term Reversal 39

8 The Science Behind Reversal–Why This Works 43

9 Your Roadmap to Diabetes Reversal –Made Simple 48

10 Your 24-Hour Diabetes Reversal Challenge 54

11 The Truth About Medications & Insulin–Are You Stuck in the Loop? 57

12 Exercise That Works–No Gym Needed! 62

13 The Stress–Diabetes Connection: How to Take Back Control 67

14 Smart Eating : Timing & Portion Control   72

15 The Hidden Truth Behind 'Healthy' Labels – Outsmarting the...   77

16 Know Yourself Before You Heal Yourself   83

17 Continuous Glucose Monitoring(CGM): Your 24/7 Blood Sugar...   89

18 Know Your Starting Line: The DIY Metabolic Checkup   93

19 Glucose in Action–Your Lifestyle Optimization Blueprint   97

20 The Insulin Upgrade: Boost Sensitivity, Reverse Faster   101

21 The Meal Order That Heals: SixthGear's Proven Sequencing...   106

22 Sweet Trap: The Bitter Truth About Artificial Sweeteners   110

23 Stress–The Silent Saboteur of Diabetes Reversal   115

24 Hydration– The Hidden Hero of Diabetes Reversal   120

25 Herbal Remedies & Diabetes: Facts, Myths & Smart Choices   124

A Message from My Heart to Yours   128

REVERSE DIABETES AND RECLAIM YOUR LIFE

Dr Mahesh Patil

Author, Mentor & Diabetes Reversal

Contact: +91 704 5544 195

Publisher: TechChase Digital Solutions

Website: www.TechChase.in

Contact: +91 8850 237 339

If you wish to gift this book to many people, we can offer you an bulk discount.

Prologue

"Health isn't simply the absence of disease — it's the presence of energy, purpose, and freedom."

A Note from the Author

This book is more than a guide — it's a reflection of real-life transformations, including my own. It's built on the courage of individuals who refused to settle for a life ruled by diabetes and dared to take their health back into their hands.

To my patients who embraced the possibility of reversal: your belief, even when the world said otherwise, has been my greatest motivation. And to those who stumbled along the way — your journey matters too. Every setback carried a lesson, and every attempt was a declaration of hope.

Diabetes may have shaped your past, but it doesn't have to define your future. The power to reclaim your health lies within you. This book is my commitment to walk beside you — with science, compassion, and an unshakable belief in your ability to heal.

Welcome to the beginning of your transformation. Let's rewrite your story — one choice at a time.

With heartfelt gratitude
Dr. Mahesh D. Patil
Author, Mentor & Diabetes Reversal Coach

"This isn't just a book. It's your roadmap to a diabetes-free life."

"Everything you've been told about diabetes isn't the whole truth. It's time to discover what they never taught you."

"To every bold soul who believed that reversal is possible — this is for you."

Introduction

About Dr. Mahesh Patil

Dr. Mahesh Patil is a highly respected Diabetes Reversal Coach and Ayurveda Physician with over two decades of clinical experience. A graduate of the prestigious **R.A. Podar Government Ayurveda College and Hospital**, he blends the ancient wisdom of Ayurveda with cutting-edge nutritional science to offer a holistic approach to diabetes management and reversal.

Dr. Patil holds a **European certification from ESPEN (Europe)** in *Nutrition Support for Metabolic Syndrome* and is a **Certified Diabetes Educator** and **Certified Diabetes Nutritionist**. He is also certified by the **American Diabetes Association** in *Diabetes Prevention* and holds various advanced credentials in **Nutrition, Nutrigenomics, Pediatric Nutrition**, and **Diabetes Nutrition**.

Adding a unique integrative dimension to his practice, Dr. Patil is also a **Certified Chakra Healing Expert**, empowering patients to align mind-body-energy for sustainable healing.

With his science-backed protocols and compassionate coaching, Dr. Mahesh Patil has helped hundreds reclaim their health and reverse diabetes naturally through the **Sixth Gear Method**.

Why This Book

Becoming a doctor wasn't just my career path — it was my calling. And for that, I owe deep gratitude to my parents, wife Dr. Archana, my teachers, and the many mentors who helped shape my journey.

It all began in 1995, when I secured admission to the prestigious R.A. Podar Ayurved Medical College in Mumbai through the merit quota. It was a proud moment — not just for me, but for my entire family. At that time, I didn't know that this step would eventually lead me to a mission far bigger than just clinical practice.

After graduation, life threw its first real challenge. My dream of pursuing a post-graduate degree had to be paused due to financial constraints. My father had retired from government service, and with limited resources, further studies seemed impossible. But where many would see an end, I saw an opening. In 2004, I returned to my hometown of Dombivli and started my own medical practice from scratch.

In those early days, something deeply disturbed me: patients, especially those newly diagnosed with diabetes, were being given prescriptions — not explanations. They were offered medications, but rarely empowered with lifestyle guidance. The focus was on treating symptoms, not on addressing the root cause.

This gap pushed me to explore deeper. Over time, I had the privilege of treating thousands of patients from diverse cultural, religious, and dietary backgrounds. One thing stood out — those who made small, consistent lifestyle changes began showing extraordinary improvements, especially in managing diabetes. That's when the question began to stir in my heart: *Could food, movement, and mindset hold the true key to diabetes reversal?*

I turned back to the foundational wisdom of Ayurveda — especially the principles of **Aahar-Vihar** (diet and lifestyle) — and began integrating it with modern science. I completed specialized training in diabetes education and clinical nutrition, refining my focus on **reversal** rather than just control. And with that, a new phase of my mission was born.

But the journey wasn't without frustration. Initially, I relied on Medical Nutrition Therapy and regular checkups. Yet many patients dropped out or lost motivation. They were overwhelmed, distracted, or simply didn't believe they could reverse diabetes. That was a turning point. I realized: *Knowledge alone isn't enough. People need systems. They need structure. They need support.*

So I built a **step-by-step, tech-enabled system** to hold patients accountable, make tracking easy, and ensure follow-through. I introduced digital tools, CGM devices, customized plans — all designed to keep patients engaged until they saw results. Because without a clear **goal**, there's no urgency. And without urgency, there's no change.

The reward? I've witnessed lives transformed. Patients who once felt doomed to a lifetime of medications have walked away free — energized, empowered, and in control. Families have celebrated, not just improved sugar levels, but restored hope.

And every message that says, *"Doctor, I never thought this was possible"* reminds me why I do what I do.

While writing this book, I often think of the story of David and Goliath — a small boy defeating a giant with nothing but faith and a sling. Diabetes may feel like a giant. But I've seen firsthand that with **discipline, clarity, and the right tools**, anyone can defeat it.

This book is my way of sharing everything I've learned. It's not theory — it's tested, practical, real-world guidance. Whether you're newly diagnosed or have struggled for years, this is your playbook to reclaim your life.

And I'll leave you with a thought from Rakesh Jhunjhunwala, the legendary Indian investor, who once said, *"My biggest mistake was not investing in my health."* Let that not be your story.

This book is your chance to invest in your health. The only question is — are you ready to begin?

1

What Is Diabetes – And Why You Can Reverse It

If you've been told the same, you're not alone. Many people feel the same confusion and fear.

For years, we've been told that diabetes is a lifelong problem. That once it starts, it never goes away. Medicines, insulin injections, sugar checks — many people feel stuck in this routine.

But here's something important:

Type 2 diabetes can be reversed.

Yes — you can get better, if you understand what's going wrong in your body and make some smart changes.

💡 So, What Is Diabetes?

When we eat food, our body turns most of it into a type of sugar called **glucose**. This glucose gives us energy.

But glucose needs to enter our body's cells. To do that, it needs help from a hormone called **insulin**, which works like a **key**. Insulin is made by an organ called the **pancreas**.

Think of it like this:

- Insulin is the **key**
- Cells are **locked doors**
- Glucose is waiting **outside the door**
- When the key (insulin) works, glucose enters the cells and gives you energy.

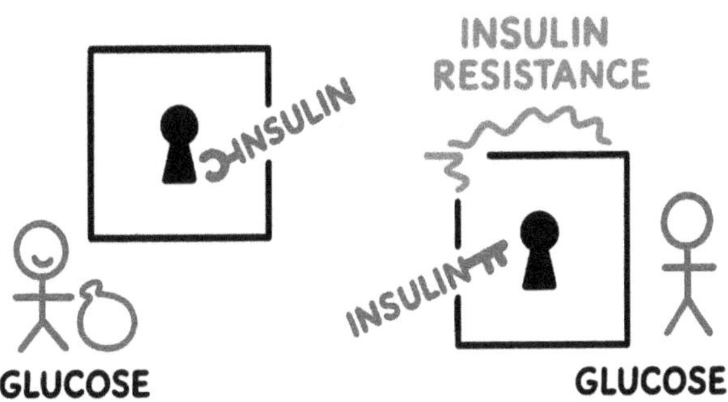

But in diabetes, this system doesn't work properly.

- Either the key doesn't fit the lock well (called **insulin resistance**)
- Or the body doesn't make enough keys (called **insulin deficiency**)

As a result, glucose stays in the blood — not in the cells. This leads to **high blood sugar** — which is what diabetes is.

🔲 Why Is Diabetes So Common Today?

500 years ago, diabetes was very rare. Our ancestors didn't count calories, didn't have diet plans, and never took insulin injections.

So, what changed?

The answer is our **modern lifestyle**:

- **Junk food**: Too much sugar, fried food, processed snacks
- **Lack of movement**: We sit too much, move too little
- **Stress and poor sleep**: Long work hours, late nights, anxiety
- **Wrong information**: People are told to manage diabetes, not reverse it

Also, let's be real — some big companies make huge money selling diabetes medicine. If people start getting cured, they lose customers. That's why the idea of "reversal" is not promoted much.

But the truth is: **You don't need to depend on medicines forever.**

You can take charge of your health. And this book will show you how.

⚖ Type 1 and Type 2 Diabetes – What's the Difference?

Type 1 diabetes is an autoimmune condition where the body's immune system attacks insulin-producing cells in the pancreas. It usually begins in childhood or adolescence and requires lifelong insulin therapy. Unlike Type 2, it is **not caused by lifestyle factors**. Currently, **Type 1 diabetes is not curable**, but it can be effectively managed with insulin, a healthy lifestyle, and regular monitoring.

There are two main types of diabetes:

- **Type 1** – This happens when the body's immune system attacks insulin-making cells. It usually starts in childhood. People with Type 1 **must take insulin**.
- **Type 2** – This is the common one, usually caused by poor lifestyle. In this, the body either doesn't use insulin well or doesn't make enough. **This type can be reversed.**

⚡ The Hidden Enemy: Insulin Resistance

Before diabetes shows up on a test report, it quietly builds up for years through a condition called **insulin resistance**.
Let's revisit the key analogy:

- In a healthy person, insulin (the key) opens the cell doors effortlessly.
- In insulin resistance, the lock is jammed. Your body needs more and more insulin to get the same job done.
- Eventually, the pancreas can't keep up. That's when sugar starts spilling over in your blood — leading to full-blown diabetes.

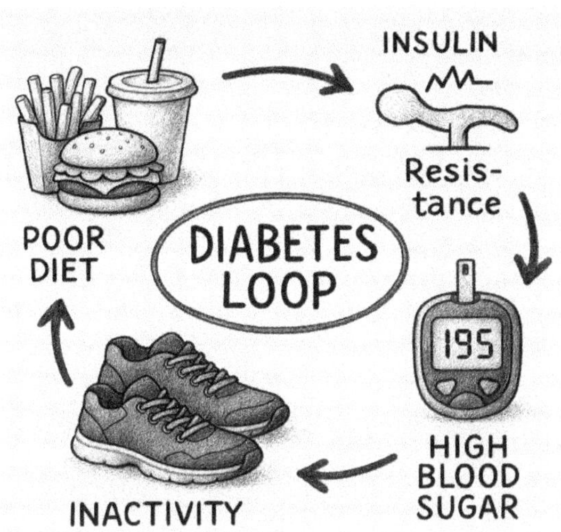

🔍 How Does a Person Become Diabetic?

It doesn't happen in one day. Diabetes builds up slowly over many years.

Here's how:
1. **Insulin resistance starts** – Your cells stop listening to insulin.
2. **Pancreas gets tired** – It works harder and harder to make more insulin.
3. **Blood sugar rises** – Glucose stays in the blood, not in cells.
4. **Symptoms appear** – Tiredness, frequent urination, thirst, blurry vision.

But don't worry — if we can understand how it started, we can also learn how to stop it.

⚠ Insulin Resistance – The Main Problem Behind Diabetes

This is the root cause of most Type 2 diabetes.
Let's understand it simply:

- Normally, insulin opens the cells and lets glucose go in.
- But in **insulin resistance**, the key (insulin) stops working well.
- So, the sugar stays in the blood and the pancreas works harder.
- Over time, this leads to **Type 2 diabetes**.

What causes insulin resistance?

- Too much sugar and junk food
- Belly fat (fat around liver and pancreas is worst)
- Sitting all day
- Poor sleep and stress
- Family history (but lifestyle still matters a lot)

🧘 What Ayurveda Says About Diabetes

In Ayurveda, diabetes is called **Madhumeha**.
It is not just a sugar problem — it is a sign of imbalance in the whole body:

- Weak digestion (low **Agni**)
- Toxin buildup (called **Ama**)
- Imbalance in **Kapha dosha** (linked to weight, laziness, mucus)
- Weak immunity (called **Ojas**)

So, the Ayurvedic view matches what modern science is now proving — diabetes starts much before blood sugar levels rise.

✅ Signs of Insulin Resistance

- Constant cravings (especially for sweets and snacks)
- Belly fat that won't go away
- Feeling tired often, even after sleeping
- Dark skin patches (on neck, underarms)
- Brain fog or poor focus

⇄ Can You Reverse Insulin Resistance?

The truth about diabetes reversal is often hidden beneath layers of outdated medical advice and pharmaceutical interests. It's suppressed by systems that profit more from lifelong management than from true healing. Many who speak of reversal are ridiculed or dismissed as unrealistic or unscientific. Yet, thousands have proven that with the right lifestyle changes, reversal *is* possible—and it's time the world knew.

Yes, you can! And that's how you reverse diabetes too.

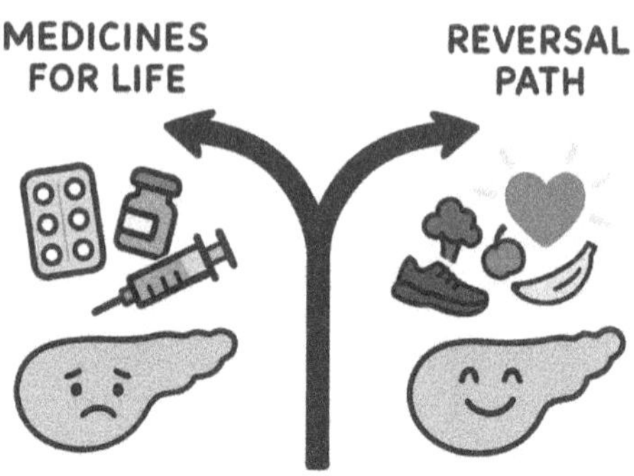

Here's how:

- ✔ **Eat right** – Less sugar, more natural food
- ✔ **Move daily** – Walk, stretch, exercise
- ✔ **Reduce stress** – Try deep breathing, meditation, yoga
- ✔ **Sleep well** – 7 to 8 hours of proper rest
- ✔ **Try fasting** (if suitable) – Give your body time to repair

Even losing **just 5 to 10% of your body weight** can make a big difference.

☆ Final Words from This Chapter

You are not powerless. Diabetes is not your destiny.

It's a signal from your body, asking for help — not a lifelong sentence. By learning what's happening inside, and making small, daily changes, **you can heal**.

Let's continue your journey in the next chapter, where I'll show you **the 6 key switches** to turn your body from disease mode to healing mode.

💬 **Your action for today:**

Just ask yourself: *What if my body actually wants to heal... and I finally give it the chance?*

2

What If Everything You Knew About Diabetes Was Wrong?

What if diabetes was never meant to be a lifelong disease? What if you've been misled — not by accident, but by design?"

Imagine waking up one day and realizing... most of what you've been told about diabetes is not true.

For years, you've heard the same things:

☞ "Diabetes is chronic."

☞ "It cannot be reversed."

☞ "You'll need medicine forever."

But here's the truth:

None of this is completely true.

Yes, diabetes is real. But the way it's explained — and the way it's treated — is one of the biggest lies in modern healthcare.

💰 Why? Because a healthy person is a lost customer.

Let's be honest. Big pharmaceutical companies don't earn money from healthy people. They grow their business when people **stay sick**, not when they get cured.

Think about it:
— Medicines, insulin, test strips, hospital visits — all create **lifelong customers**.
— If people started reversing diabetes, that entire industry would collapse.

That's why the truth about reversal is hidden. Suppressed. Even ridiculed.
But not anymore.

This chapter is your **RED PILL MOMENT** — once you know the truth, you'll never see diabetes the same way again. You'll stop thinking of it as a disease, and start understanding it as a **result of wrong inputs**. And the best part? **You can change those inputs.**

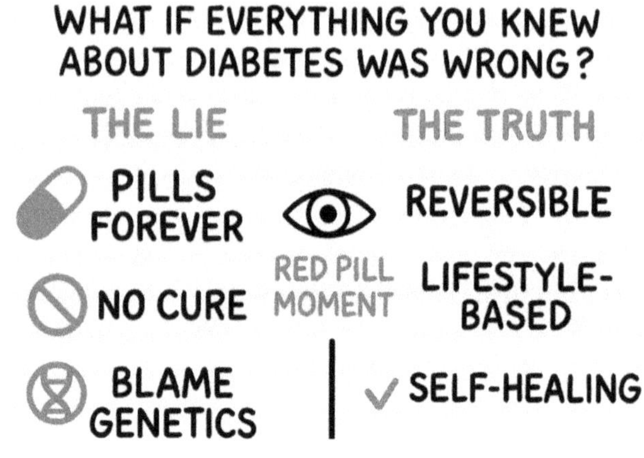

500 Years Ago – A World Without Diabetes

Close your eyes and imagine:

- No fast food
- No sugary drinks
- No late-night TV or phone scrolling
- People walking, farming, living with nature
- Food that came from farms, not factories

Back then, people didn't need pills or insulin. Why? Because **their lifestyle kept them naturally healthy**.

So what changed?

1. Processed food became common — full of sugar, chemicals, and artificial ingredients
2.Movement disappeared — we stopped walking, started sitting

3. Stress increased, and **sleep got worse** — hormones went out of balance

4. The Pharma industry grew — and saw diabetes as a long-term business

Let's be real:

Have you ever seen a big campaign promoting diabetes reversal?

Why don't doctors talk about reversing diabetes, only managing it?

Despite medical advancements, why are diabetes cases going UP, not down?

Because there's **more money in keeping you sick than in helping you heal.**

🐘 The Big Diabetes Scam – How You Were Kept in the Dark

Let's bust the 3 biggest lies you've been told:

"Diabetes is genetic."

✓ Truth: Only about 5% of cases are truly genetic. The rest are due to food, lifestyle, and stress.

"You'll need medicine for life."

✓ Truth: Medicines only control sugar. They don't cure the root cause. That's why doses keep increasing.

"Diabetes cannot be reversed."

✓ Truth: Thousands of people have reversed it by changing what they eat, how they move, and how they live.

🔖 How They Keep You Trapped

Here's how the diabetes industry works:

1. They call diabetes "incurable"
2. They give you sugar-lowering drugs that only manage symptoms
3. They hide or ignore studies that show lifestyle changes can reverse it
4. They sponsor research that favors pills over natural healing

The result?

A world full of patients stuck in a **loop of medicines**, thinking that's the only way to survive.

But not you.

You're about to break free.

🔓 The Sixth Gear Code – Your Path to Freedom

Here's the empowering truth:

✔ You are not weak.

✔ Your body is not broken.

✔ Your diabetes is not permanent.

Your body is just **reacting to the wrong inputs** — and the moment you fix them, your body will start healing. It's waiting for your permission.

🔥 In this book, you will learn:

- How to reset your blood sugar naturally
- What to eat (and what to avoid) to heal your body
- Why movement, not just exercise, is powerful
- How stress, sleep, and emotions impact your sugar levels

- A clear action plan to reverse diabetes and take charge of your health

If you're tired of pills, tired of fear, tired of feeling helpless — you're in the right place.
This is your turning point. Your comeback story starts now.

3

How Diabetes Can Actually Be Reversed

When you hear the word **"reversal,"** what comes to your mind?
- Expensive treatments?
- Some new magic medicine?
- Strict diets that make life miserable?

Let's clear one thing right now:

Reversing diabetes is not magic — it's science.

It's about **understanding how your body works** and helping it do what it was designed to do: **heal itself.**

💡 So, What's the Real Problem in Diabetes?

At the root of Type 2 diabetes is something called **insulin resistance**.

Normally, insulin acts like a key. It opens the doors of your cells so that sugar (glucose) from your food can go inside and give you energy.

But when you have insulin resistance, the key doesn't work well.

The door remains closed.

Sugar stays in your blood.

Your body keeps making more and more insulin — but it doesn't help.

✔ The Good News: Insulin Resistance Can Be Reversed

Yes, instead of just **controlling sugar with medicines**, you can actually **fix the root problem** by making some lifestyle changes.

Your body is not broken — it's just **overloaded**.

And when you remove the wrong inputs (like junk food, too much sitting, too much stress), your body starts to work properly again.

Your Body Is a Self-Healing Machine

Your body is always working in the background — healing, repairing, and balancing things.

Here's how your body can reverse diabetes naturally:

🔑 1. Improve Insulin Sensitivity

When your cells become sensitive again, they respond better to insulin. That means sugar can enter cells and blood sugar levels come down. You can do this through:

- Eating real, clean food

- Regular movement
- Staying away from refined carbs and sugary drinks

🔥 2. Reduce Inflammation

Inflammation is like a silent fire inside your body — it blocks healing. It's caused by:

- Processed food
- Stress
- Lack of sleep
- Toxins

By reducing inflammation, your insulin starts working better again.

⚖️ 3. Balance Your Hormones

Hormones like **cortisol** (from stress) and **growth hormone** affect your sugar levels.

Too much stress = too much cortisol = more sugar in the blood.

Fix your sleep, reduce stress, do breathing exercises — and your hormones will balance out.

💪 Your Body Wants to Heal. Let It.

Think about this:

– Cut your finger → body heals.
– Catch a cold → body fights back.
– Eat the wrong food → body tries to detox.

So why can't your body fix insulin resistance too?

It can — if you give it the right tools.

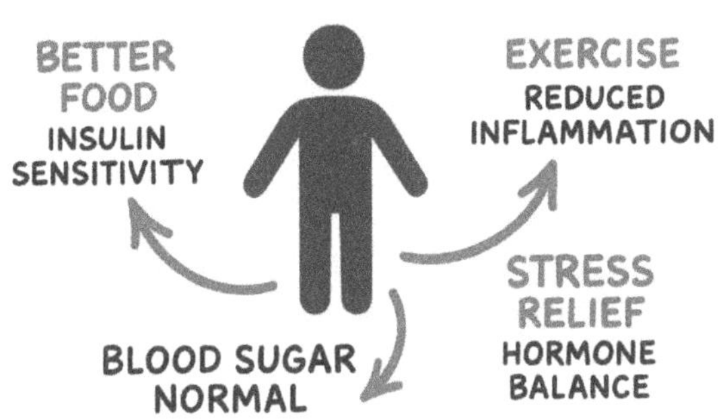

Reversal is not about perfection.

It's about **small, consistent changes** that your body loves.

It won't happen overnight — but in just a few weeks, you can feel more energy, better sugar levels, and real hope.

And don't worry — you're not alone. I'll walk you through it.

In the next chapters, you'll learn:

- What foods to eat
- How to move your body
- Simple stress-reducing habits

These are not fancy tricks — they're **simple science-backed steps anyone can follow.**

4

Eat to Heal – The Diabetes Reversal Diet

Most people think food is just something you eat to fill your stomach or give you energy. But when it comes to **reversing diabetes**, food becomes something far more powerful.

The right food can:

✔ Improve insulin sensitivity

✔ Lower inflammation

✔ Balance your hormones

✔ Reset your metabolism

Sounds magical? It's not. It's **science** — and the good news is, it works.

🥦 Eat the Foods That Heal

Let's start with the most important rule:
Don't focus on eating less. Focus on eating right.
Here are the 4 food principles you must follow:

1. Low-Carb, High-Fiber Foods

Carbohydrates (especially refined ones) raise your blood sugar quickly. But fiber slows things down.
Eat more:

- Leafy greens (spinach, methi, coriander)
- Broccoli, cauliflower, cabbage
- Cucumber, karela, and bottle gourd
- Low-sugar fruits like berries or guava

These foods **don't spike your sugar** and help your cells respond better to insulin.

2. Healthy Fats Are Your Friend

Yes, you read that right — fat is not the enemy.
Good fats help:

- Reduce inflammation
- Support hormone balance
- Keep you feeling full

Add these to your meals:

- Avocado
- Olive oil or groundnut oil (cold-pressed)
- Almonds, walnuts, flaxseeds, chia seeds
- Homemade coconut chutney

3. Protein Builds & Protects

Protein helps repair cells and muscles — and that's very important for diabetics.
Include:

- Eggs, fish, chicken (lean cuts)
- Paneer, tofu
- Dal, sprouts, and lentils
- Greek yogurt (unsweetened)

Protein keeps you full and **prevents those 5 PM snack cravings** that can derail your progress.

4. Intermittent Fasting (IF)

Don't be scared of the word "fasting." It doesn't mean starving — it means eating within a set time window and letting your body rest and repair.
For example:

- Eat between 10 AM and 6 PM
- Fast from 6 PM to 10 AM the next day

Benefits of IF:

- Lowers insulin levels
- Burns fat more effectively
- Gives the pancreas a break

Always check with your doctor if you're on insulin or heavy meds before starting.

♈ You're Not Just Eating — You're Healing

When you eat with intention, every bite becomes a **step toward reversal.**

You are telling your body:

"I trust you to heal. And I will support you."

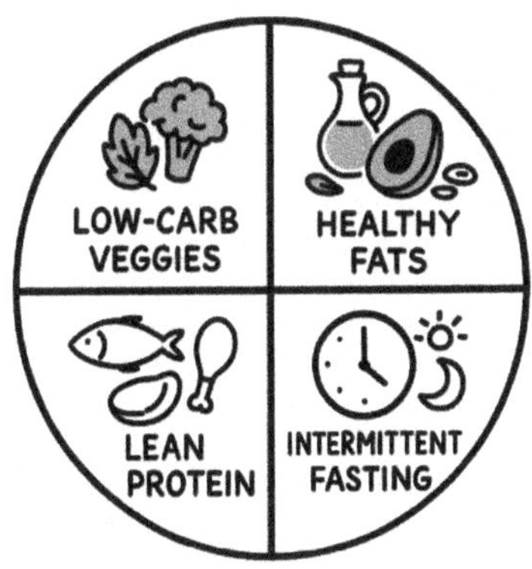

Let food be your medicine

No need to fear about food anymore. It's not about cutting everything out.

It's about **choosing food that loves you back.**

5

Move to Heal – How Exercise Reverses Diabetes

You don't need to run a marathon. You just need to move — every single day."

Exercise is one of the **most powerful tool** for reversing Type 2 diabetes.

But wait — this is not about joining a gym or sweating buckets.

This is about **daily movement**, consistency, and choosing the kind of activity your body enjoys and responds to.

When you move your body:

✔ Your muscles use up sugar for energy

✔ Blood sugar levels come down

✔ Your body becomes more sensitive to insulin

✔ Fat starts melting away

✔ Inflammation goes down

All of this adds up to one thing: **healing from the inside out.**

1. Consistency Over Intensity

You don't need to exercise hard — you just need to **move regularly**.
Try this:

- 30 minutes walk after meals
- Brisk walking, cycling, or swimming
- Dancing or even household work

Even **a 10-minute walk after lunch** can significantly reduce blood sugar spikes!

2. Strength Training: Build Muscle, Burn Sugar

Muscles are like sugar-burning machines. The more muscle you have, the more glucose your body uses — even when you're resting!
Do strength training 2–3 times a week:

- Bodyweight squats or lunges
- Resistance bands
- Push-ups or dumbbell lifts
- Climbing stairs

Don't worry — you don't need a gym. Just use your body.

3. HIIT – Quick and Powerful

HIIT means short bursts of intense effort, followed by rest.
Example:

- 30 seconds jumping jacks → 30 seconds rest
- Repeat for 15–20 minutes

HIIT is super effective for **fat burning, improving insulin**, and boosting your metabolism.

4. Movement Throughout the Day

Exercise isn't just about "workouts."
Try this:

- Walk while talking on the phone
- Do stretches during TV ads
- Use stairs instead of lift
- Sit less, move more

Every small movement adds up. Your **body was designed to move.**

5. Anti-Gravity Exercises – A Hidden Gem

Most people haven't heard of this, but **anti-gravity exercises** are amazing for reversing diabetes.
These exercises include:

- Yoga poses like **Downward Dog**, **Standing Forward Bend**,

or **Legs-Up-the-Wall**
- Using an **inversion table** to tilt your body upside down
- Practicing **Aerial Yoga** using a hammock

Benefits:

- Boosts blood circulation
- Stimulates the **lymphatic system** (removes toxins)
- Helps the **pancreas** work better
- Improves **insulin sensitivity**
- Relieves stress

Even 5–10 minutes a day of anti-gravity poses can be powerful.

◉ Bottom Line: Find What You Love

You don't have to suffer through workouts.

If you enjoy dancing, trekking, playing badminton, or gardening — that counts too!

> The more you enjoy it, the more likely you are to stick with it.
> The more you move, the better your sugar stays in control.

6

Stress & Sleep — The Hidden Keys to Healing

You may be doing everything right with food and exercise — but if stress and sleep are ignored, healing will slow down."

When it comes to reversing diabetes, most people talk about diet and exercise.

But two **equally powerful tools** often get ignored:
Stress management and **quality sleep.**

Why do they matter?

Because both **directly affect your blood sugar, hormones, and healing process**.

Even a perfect diet can't make up for **high stress and poor sleep.**

Stress – The Silent Blocker

When you're stressed, your body releases a hormone called **cortisol**.

It's helpful in emergencies — but harmful when it's always present.

Chronic stress leads to:

- Increased blood sugar
- Insulin resistance
- Belly fat
- Poor decision-making around food

Over time, stress can **undo all the benefits of your healthy habits.**

✅ How to Lower Stress Naturally

You don't need hours of therapy. Just start with these simple daily practices:

🧘 Mindfulness or Meditation (10–15 mins/day)
Deep breathing, guided meditations, or even chanting — these activate your body's **healing state** and lower cortisol.

🏃 Move Your Body
Exercise is not just for weight loss — it's one of the best **stress relievers**. Even a 15-minute walk helps.

🎵 Relax Your Mind
Do what makes you feel calm — music, nature, prayer, or reading. Even sitting quietly with your eyes closed for 5 minutes can make a difference.

zz Sleep – Your Body's Night Shift

Think of sleep as your body's time to **repair, reset, and recharge.**
During sleep:

- Your body repairs tissues
- Blood sugar stabilizes
- Insulin becomes more effective
- Hormones rebalance

Poor sleep leads to:

- Increased hunger and cravings
- Low energy
- Higher blood sugar
- Reduced willpower and mood

How to Sleep Better and Heal Faster

⏰ Stick to a Sleep Schedule
Go to bed and wake up at the same time every day — even on weekends.

🚫 Avoid Late-Night Stimulation
No screens, caffeine, or heavy food before bed. Your mind needs a wind-down routine.

🧘 Do Bedtime Rituals
Try a warm bath, light stretches, soft music, or breathing exercises.

Create a Sleep Sanctuary
Keep your bedroom dark, quiet, and cool. Use comfortable bedding. Remove distractions.

♻ The Power of Both — Stress + Sleep

Think of stress and sleep as **invisible teammates** in your diabetes reversal journey.

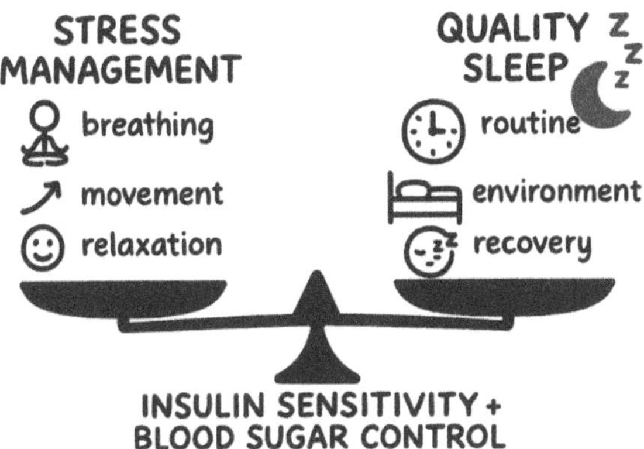

If they're not managed, they'll quietly slow your progress — no matter how good your diet is.

But when they're balanced, your body becomes a **healing machine**.

7

Habits That Heal – The Secret to Long-Term Reversal

Reversing diabetes is not about doing something once and expecting a miracle.

It's about creating **daily habits** that help your body stay healthy for the long run.

This is not a short-term fix. This is a **lifestyle transformation**.

And the real magic? It's found in **small steps, done consistently.**

✔ How to Build Habits That Stick

Here are six practical strategies that will help you stay on track and reverse diabetes for life:

1. Start Small, Stay Consistent

Don't try to change your entire life overnight.
  Start with one small habit, like:

- 10 minutes of walking daily
- Cutting one sugary snack
- Sleeping 30 minutes earlier

Once this feels easy, add the next.

2. Make It Enjoyable

Hate boring workouts? Then don't do them!
  Love dancing, yoga, or badminton? Do that instead!
  When you enjoy the process, you'll never feel like quitting.
  Healthy food can be delicious. Movement can be fun.

3. Accountability Changes Everything

Share your goals with someone.
  Better yet, find a buddy or a coach.
  When someone checks in on you — you'll stay more focused.
  Celebrate small wins together!

4. Track Your Progress

Keep a simple notebook, calendar, or use an app.
  Log your:

- Food

- Exercise
- Blood sugar levels
- Sleep & stress

It keeps you motivated when you **see progress** over time.

5. Be Patient, Stay Persistent

You didn't get diabetes in one day — so don't expect it to go away in a week.
There will be tough days. But don't quit.
Every healthy choice is a step toward reversal.
Keep showing up for yourself.

6. Build a Support System

Surround yourself with people who understand your journey.
A WhatsApp group, a local wellness circle, or even an online tribe can uplift you.
When you feel supported, **you grow faster**.

☆ Success Story: Ms. Darshana's Journey to Health

Let me share a story that gives me goosebumps every time.
Darshana was just 17.
Obese. Prediabetic. Stressed. Exhausted.
Her doctor warned: "You're on the path to type 2 diabetes."
But Darshana was ready for change.
Together, we built a plan:

- Yoga + Mindfulness to manage her stress

- Anti-gravity workouts and posture-based movement
- Colorful plates full of whole foods
- No restriction, just awareness

She showed up. Every day.

Even with her school pressure, she stuck to the process.

And guess what?

✓ In 90 days, she reversed her prediabetes

✓ Lost weight

✓ Felt energetic and in control

✓ Developed confidence that changed her life

Her story is proof that **age doesn't matter — mindset does**.

And that consistent action leads to lasting transformation.

8

The Science Behind Reversal – Why This Works

When you understand how your body works, you no longer feel helpless.

You begin to realize: *healing is possible — not by chance, but by choice.*

This chapter breaks down the **science behind how diabetes reversal works**, step-by-step. Once you know this, everything else in this book will make even more sense.

⚡ It All Starts with Insulin Resistance

Let's go back to the root problem:

Insulin is a hormone that helps sugar (glucose) enter your body's cells. This sugar gives you energy.

But in **Type 2 diabetes**, your cells stop responding to insulin.

It's like the lock isn't opening anymore, even if you have the key.

So:

- Glucose stays in the blood
- Blood sugar levels rise
- The pancreas makes more insulin
- The cycle continues...

> But here's the hope: **This insulin resistance can be reversed.**

Your body is adaptable.

When you change the inputs — your food, movement, rest, and stress — your cells become sensitive to insulin again.

🍲 Diet: The Fuel That Fixes

The food you eat either helps or harms your insulin.

✓ Whole foods like veggies, protein, healthy fats, and low-sugar fruits **lower blood sugar and heal cells**

✗ Processed carbs and sugary foods **worsen insulin resistance**

Eating real, nourishing food:

- Repairs damaged cells
- Regulates blood sugar
- Restores hormone balance

Every good meal is a message to your body:

> "It's safe to heal now."

🏃 Exercise: The Glucose Burner

When you move your body, your muscles pull glucose out of your blood and use it for energy.

This improves:

- **Insulin sensitivity**
- **Metabolism**
- **Weight loss**

Even simple activities like walking, yoga, or anti-gravity exercises create powerful changes inside your body.

Stress: The Hidden Spike

Stress causes your body to release **cortisol**, the stress hormone.

And cortisol **raises blood sugar** — even if you haven't eaten anything!

Chronic stress keeps sugar levels high, tires your pancreas, and increases insulin resistance.

Breathing exercises, nature walks, music, or meditation can:

- Lower cortisol
- Stabilize blood sugar
- Calm your nervous system

Sleep: The Reset Button

Sleep is when your body repairs itself.

Poor sleep leads to:

- Sugar cravings
- Higher blood sugar
- Fat storage
- Low energy

But when you get **7–9 hours of quality sleep**, your body:

- Restores hormones
- Improves insulin sensitivity
- Regulates appetite

⚡ The Real Magic: When It All Comes Together

Each of these — diet, movement, stress, and sleep — is powerful on its own.
But when you combine them?
That's when the **reversal process accelerates.**

> You reprogram your metabolism.
> Your cells start responding to insulin.
> Blood sugar levels drop naturally.
> And your energy, confidence, and health come back.

The science is solid.
The system works.
And now — **you know how to work with it.**

DIABETES
REVERSAL
DIET
EXERCISE
STRESS
RELIEF
SLEEP
Insulin
Sensitivity
Glucose
Use
Hormone
Balance
Cellular
Repair

9

Your Roadmap to Diabetes Reversal – Made Simple

Now that you know how diabetes really works, let's move from understanding to action. This chapter gives you a clear, simple guide to start reversing diabetes using real food, positive habits, and ancient wisdom backed by science.

Fix Your Diet – The Foundation of Healing

Your food choices control nearly 80% of your success in reversing diabetes. That's why the first step is to remove what's hurting you and replace it with what heals you.

✔ What to Eat More Of:

- **Non-starchy veggies** (spinach, cabbage, broccoli, karela)
- **Lean proteins** (chicken, fish, paneer, tofu, lentils)
- **Healthy fats** (avocado, groundnut oil, olive oil, coconut)
- **Low-GI fruits** (berries, guava, apples, pear)

✕ What to Eat Less Of:

- White rice, white bread, sugar, refined wheat flour
- Processed snacks, biscuits, namkeen, soft drinks

Understanding Glycemic Index (GI)

The **Glycemic Index (GI)** shows how fast a food raises your blood sugar. The lower the GI, the better it is for you.

- **High GI Foods**: White rice, white bread, sugar – cause sugar spikes
- **Low GI Foods**: Millets, vegetables, legumes – release sugar slowly

Carbs: Good vs Bad

- **Simple carbs** (white bread, sugar, noodles): digest fast, spike sugar
- **Complex carbs** (millets, legumes, brown rice): digest slow, give energy without sugar rush

Fiber – The Blood Sugar Shield

Fiber slows sugar absorption and improves digestion. There are two types:

- **Soluble fiber**: oats, chia, apples – forms a gel that slows sugar entry
- **Insoluble fiber**: leafy greens, nuts – supports gut health and clean bowels

Aim for 25–30g of fiber daily. It helps with weight loss, sugar control, and gut health.

Protein – Your Body's Repair System

Protein keeps you full, prevents sugar spikes, and builds lean muscle:

- Chicken, fish, eggs
- Tofu, paneer, lentils, chickpeas
- Add protein to every meal

Healthy Fats – Hormone Support + Energy

Good fats reduce inflammation and help insulin work better:

- Avocado, olive oil, flaxseeds, walnuts, chia seeds
- Omega-3s from fish (salmon, sardines)

The Big Myth: "No Rice, More Wheat"

Many think skipping rice and eating more wheat is the solution. But truth is:

- **Refined wheat** (white bread, roti) = high GI
- **Brown rice, millets** = lower GI, more fiber, better sugar control

Positive Millets - The Diabetes Superstars

Let's look at a simplified table:

Nutrient	Barnyard Millet	Foxtail Millet	White Rice	Wheat
Glycemic Index	50-55 (Low)	50-55 (Low)	73-85	70-75
Protein (g)	6.2	12.3	6.8	11.8
Fiber (g)	9.8	•80	0.6	2.0
Iron (mg)	4.2	2.8	0.8	3.9
Magnesium (mg)	85	81	19	43

Sixth Gear Millet Protocol:

- Start with **Barnyard Millet** (unpolished, soaked for 8+ hrs)
- Cook 1:2 with water like rice
- Replace white rice or wheat for 1–2 meals daily
- In 90 days: Up to 2.5% drop in HbA1c observed in many patients

Positive vs Neutral vs Negative Grains

Category	Examples
✅ Positive Millets	Barnyard, Foxtail, Kodo, Little millet
⚖️ Neutral Grains	Oats, Barley, Quinoa, Ragi, Bajra, Jowar
❌ Negative Grains	White rice, White bread, Maida-based snacks

Positive Mindset + Support

You're not just changing food. You're changing beliefs, emotions, and daily habits. That's why coaching helps you:

- Unlearn myths
- Build trust in your body
- Stay consistent through doubt

At Sixth Gear, I've guided everyone from students to surgeons. Many reversed their diabetes not just with food, but with faith.

Fiber-Rich Foods to Add Daily:

- Millets: barnyard, foxtail, finger millet
- Legumes: lentils, beans, chickpeas
- Vegetables: spinach, broccoli, carrots
- Fruits: apples, pears, berries
- Seeds: chia, flax, pumpkin
- Nuts: almonds, walnuts

Final Word: Start With Food

If you do just one thing today, let it be this: **Replace your high-GI grains with unpolished millets.** It's simple, affordable, and backed by science. The road to diabetes freedom starts in your kitchen.

Ready for the next step? Let's move forward!

6 PILLARS OF DIABETES REVERSAL

❶ PILLAR 1
CHANGE YOUR DIET

Focus on vegetables, lean proteins, healthy fats, low-glycemic fruits

❷ EXERCISE

Engage in regular physical activity

❸ MANAGE STRESS

Practice relaxation techniques

❹ IMPROVE SLEEP

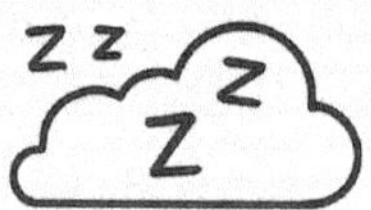

Get adequate, quality sleep

❺ INCREASE FIBER INTAKE

Eat more high-fiber foods

❻ REDUCE MEDICATION

Safely lower use of diabetes drugs

10

Your 24-Hour Diabetes Reversal Challenge

"The journey to health begins with a single, small step."

To truly transform your health, you need momentum.

And momentum doesn't come from thinking — it comes from doing.

So here's your first **Reversal Challenge.**

Do it today. Do it now. Let's build momentum.

24-Hour Challenge: Start Your Reversal Engine

For the next 24 hours, follow these 3 powerful steps:

✓ **Swap refined grains**

- ✗ White rice, maida, bread
- ✓ Use brown rice, unpolished barnyard millet, or whole wheat chapati

✓ Add 1 liter of extra water

- Hydration flushes toxins and helps control blood sugar

✓ Walk for 10 minutes after one meal

- A short walk after eating helps reduce sugar spikes!

◉ **Goal:** Just do **one** of these steps today. Even that is enough to start your reversal engine!

🥷 Set Your Personal WHY

If you want to stay consistent on this journey, define your **emotional reason** — your **"why."**

Write it down. Look at it often.

☞ **Why do you want to reverse diabetes?**

☑ To stop medications?

☑ To avoid complications like nerve damage or heart issues?

☑ To feel younger and more energetic?

☑ To live long for your kids, partner, or family?

✍ **My reason for reversing diabetes is:**

____

____

____

____

Whenever you feel tired or doubt yourself — come back to this page and read your WHY.

"Your reason is more powerful than any excuse."

🎉 This Is Just the Beginning!

You've already done something 99% of people don't:

You've read, reflected, and taken a decision to take control.

Now, let's build on this action.

In the next sections, we'll unlock more powerful tools and strategies that will take your reversal journey to the next level.

Ready to rise?

Let's go! 🔥

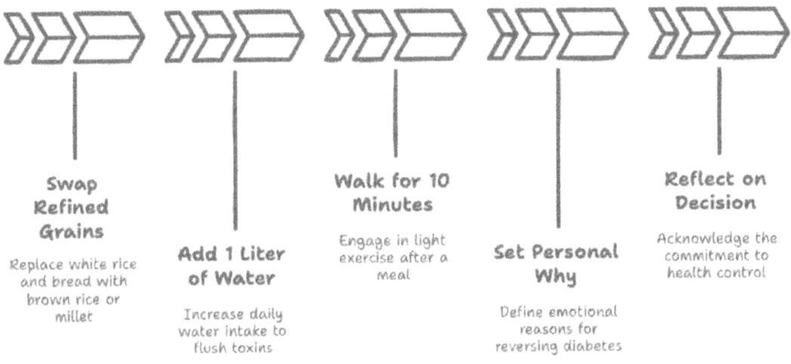

11

The Truth About Medications & Insulin – Are You Stuck in the Loop?

"You'll need these medicines for life." That's what most people are told the moment they're diagnosed with diabetes. And just like that, they start a journey of pills, injections, and increasing dosages—without ever questioning why. But what if that's only half the truth?

Let's break it down:

🔖 **Diabetes medications do NOT cure diabetes.**

They only manage the symptoms while the root cause silently gets worse.

And the worst part? Over time, you may need stronger drugs, higher doses, and eventually—insulin.

So, how do you break free from this medication trap?

Let's start with how these drugs actually work.

🔍 What Diabetes Medications Really Do

Here are the five main types of diabetes medications—and the hidden truths behind each:

Metformin – Reduces sugar production in the liver.
⚠ Can cause vitamin B12 deficiency over time, leading to nerve issues.

Sulfonylureas (e.g., Glimepiride) – Push the pancreas to release more insulin.
⚠ *Can exhaust your pancreas, making you insulin-dependent faster.*

SGLT-2 Inhibitors (e.g., Dapagliflozin) – Make you pee out extra sugar.
⚠ *Risk of dehydration and urinary infections.*

DPP-4 Inhibitors (e.g., Sitagliptin) – Help manage insulin after meals.
⚠ *Linked to potential pancreatic issues in some cases.*

Insulin Injections – Often prescribed when nothing else works.
⚠ *Adding more insulin doesn't fix insulin resistance. In fact, it can make it worse.*

☞ **Pattern alert**: These medications **don't treat the real issue—insulin resistance.** They only mask symptoms.

⇋ Why Do You Keep Needing More?

Doctors increase your medication dose because your body becomes more resistant to insulin. Why?

- ❗ You're not addressing the root cause (insulin resistance)
- ❗ Your body adapts, so the same dose stops working
- ❗ Medications give a false sense of safety, so lifestyle changes are ignored

This creates a **dangerous cycle** where you become more dependent instead of less.

But here's the truth:

🧠 **Diabetes is a lifestyle condition—and that means it can be reversed with lifestyle too.**

✔ Can You Reduce or Stop Medications?

Yes! But it must be done safely and systematically.

Here's the three-step process we use at Sixth Gear:

⚡ Step 1: Fix Your Food First

- Eliminate sugar and refined carbs
- Eat high-fiber foods, good fats, and clean proteins
- Add gut-healing foods to reduce inflammation

💪 Step 2: Move with Purpose

- Use strength training and anti-gravity exercises
- Walk for 10 minutes after meals (yes, it works!)
- Stay consistent with light movement throughout the day

📊 Step 3: Monitor Closely

- Track your sugar levels daily
- Adjust medication with your doctor's help
- Use CGM (Continuous Glucose Monitor) if possible

Many of my clients have reduced or stopped insulin completely within 90 days using this exact method.

Medications vs. Reversal — Your Final Choice

Let's be clear:

- **Medications are not the enemy.**
- But they are not your freedom either.

They are tools. And tools should help you get better—not trap you in a loop.

*The real solution lies in fixing your **insulin resistance**, not in increasing your insulin dose.*

🔥 So here's your moment of choice:

- 💊 Continue depending on medications forever
- **OR**
- 👟 Start reversing diabetes with food, movement, sleep, and mindset

What will you choose?

The pill path... or the healing path?

Your body already knows the answer. Let's help it win.

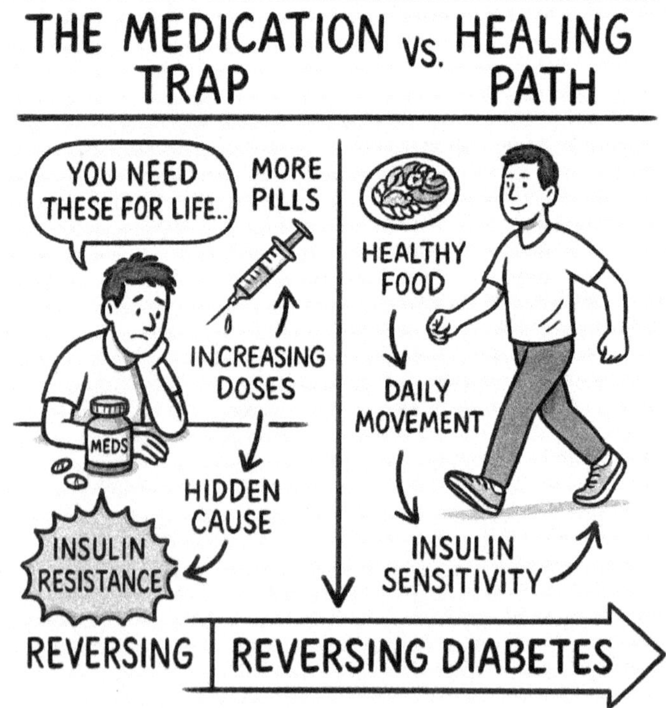

12

Exercise That Works – No Gym Needed!

Sound familiar? You're not alone.

Most people with diabetes **struggle with exercise** because they think they need long, tiring workouts

- Believe walking is enough
- Don't know which exercises actually help with sugar control

But here's the truth:

Diabetes isn't just about burning calories.

It's about fixing **insulin resistance.**

And the fastest way to do that is through **targeted move‑ment**—not hours at the gym.

Why Walking Alone Isn't Enough

Walking is good—but not enough to reverse diabetes on its own. Why?

Because it doesn't wake up your **biggest sugar-absorbing muscles.**

Imagine your muscles are like a sponge:

- After meals, they soak up sugar from your blood.
- But if you don't use them enough, they go dry and stiff.
- Sugar stays in the blood = high sugar levels = more insulin needed.

Solution?

✓ Build muscle strength
✓ Move big muscles (legs, hips, glutes)
✓ Improve insulin sensitivity
☞ Enter **Anti-Gravity Exercises!**

💪 What Are Anti-Gravity Exercises?

These are easy, low-impact moves that **use your own body weight** to fight gravity.

They don't need equipment, don't strain your joints, and take just minutes!

Even 10 minutes a day can make a BIG impact!

🔥 3 Anti-Gravity Exercises That Lower Sugar Naturally

1. Wall Sit – The Sugar Burner

- Stand with your back against the wall
- Slide down till your knees are at 90° (like sitting on an invisible chair)
- Hold for 30–60 seconds
- Repeat 2–3 rounds

💡 *Activates thighs and glutes—the biggest sugar-absorbing muscles in your body.*

2. Calf Raises – Boost Blood Flow & Glucose Use

- Stand tall, feet hip-width apart
- Rise up on your toes, hold 1 sec, slowly come down
- Do 15–20 reps

💡 *Improves circulation, strengthens muscles, helps sugar enter cells faster.*

3. Seated Leg Lifts – Simple Yet Powerful

- Sit on a chair, back straight
- Lift one leg, hold for 5 seconds, lower
- Repeat 10 times per leg

💡 *Great for beginners. Strengthens core, supports better sugar balance.*

🔲 The 10-Minute Daily Plan

◈ **Morning** – 2 Rounds of Wall Sit
◈ **Afternoon** – 20 Calf Raises
◈ **Evening** – 10 Seated Leg Lifts

- **Bonus:** Take a 10-minute walk after lunch or dinner to stop sugar spikes.

Real Results from Real People

> "I just did these 10-minute moves at home—and my sugar dropped 50 points!"
> – **Rajesh, 52**, *diabetes reversed in 90 days*

These aren't workouts.

These are **sugar-control power moves** for busy people like you.

✔ Your 7-Day Challenge

🖉 *Commit just 10 minutes a day*

🖉 *Track your sugar before and after*

🖉 *Feel stronger, more energetic, and in control!*

You don't need the gym.
You just need the right movements.
Let's move—one day at a time—toward a diabetes-free life.

13

The Stress–Diabetes Connection: How to Take Back Control

You may not realize it, but **stress alone** can raise your blood sugar—even if you haven't eaten anything!

Imagine this:

- You wake up and check your sugar—it looks normal.
- Then you get into an argument, read a stressful email, or get stuck in traffic.
- By afternoon, your sugar has shot up—even though you ate healthy all day.

Why does this happen?

How Stress Spikes Blood Sugar

When you're stressed, your brain thinks you're in danger.

To help you "escape," it triggers the **fight-or-flight response**, releasing stress hormones like **cortisol and adrenaline.**

These hormones flood your blood with glucose to give you quick energy—even though there's no real danger to run from.

But here's the problem: You're just sitting at your desk, in a car, or lying in bed. And the sugar stays in your blood.

💡 *Fact: Chronic stress makes you more insulin resistant, causing constant sugar spikes—even if your diet is perfect.*

🧘 5 Simple Ways to Beat Stress & Lower Sugar

These science-backed habits can help **calm your mind and your blood sugar.**

1. The 60-Second Sugar Reset (Breathing Exercise)

Just one minute of calm breathing can lower cortisol instantly.
Try this:
  Inhale through your nose – 4 seconds
  ✋ Hold your breath – 7 seconds
  =3 Exhale slowly – 8 seconds
  ↩ Repeat 4 rounds
  ✒ *Why it works:* This breathing activates your **vagus nerve**—telling your body to relax and lower sugar.

2. The "Stress Detox" Journal

Writing can release mental stress and help your brain shift focus.
Each night, write down:
  ✔ 3 good things that happened
  ✔ 1 stressful thing (and why)
  ✔ 1 action to make tomorrow better

🖋 *Why it works:* Writing helps clear your mind and lowers negative emotions that fuel sugar spikes.

3. Nature – The Original Insulin

A few minutes in nature can reset your hormones!
Try to:
🌿 Walk barefoot on grass
☀ Sit in sunlight for 10 mins
🌳 Be near trees or plants
🖋 *Why it works:* Studies show nature reduces stress hormones by up to 30%, helping control sugar naturally.

4. Laughter Therapy – The Best Free Medicine

Laughing isn't just fun—it's therapeutic!
 Watch comedy clips or funny videos
👨‍👩‍👧‍👦 Spend time with light-hearted people
🧘 Try laughter yoga (10 mins = real benefits)
🖋 *Why it works:* Laughter releases **endorphins**, lowers cortisol, and boosts insulin sensitivity.

5. The Hand Massage Trick (Instant Relief)

Need to relax quickly? Try this 2-minute trick.
✋ Rub your palms together for 30 seconds
👐 Then massage the soft spot between your thumb and index finger
😌 Repeat twice a day—or whenever you feel tense
🖋 *Why it works:* This pressure point calms the nervous system and supports healthy circulation.

💬 Real Story: How Meena Lowered Her Sugar

"I always thought my food was the issue. But when I started focusing on stress, my fasting sugar dropped from 180 to 130—without changing my diet!"
— Meena, 53

◉ 7-Day Stress-Lowering Challenge

Take this one-week challenge and track your sugar before and after:
- ✔ 4-7-8 breathing – 2x daily
- ✔ Journal before bed
- ✔ Spend 10 minutes in nature
- ✔ Laugh at least once every day
- ✔ Do the hand massage when stressed

Watch how your sugar drops—even without changing your food!

✔ *Final Thought: Calm Mind = Controlled Sugar*

Food matters. But if you ignore stress, your sugar may stay high—no matter how healthy you eat.

Calm your mind.
Take small daily steps.
And give your body the peace it needs to heal.

LOWER BLOOD SUGAR NATURALLY

14

Smart Eating: Timing & Portion Control

Why *When* You Eat Matters as Much as *What* You Eat

Most people worry only about what food to eat. But here's the truth: **Even healthy food, if eaten at the wrong time or in large amounts, can raise your blood sugar.**

If you want to reverse diabetes, **timing and quantity** are just as important as quality.

⏰ The Science Behind Meal Timing

Your body follows a natural clock, called the **circadian rhythm**. If you eat according to this clock, your insulin works better. But eating too late or at odd times can confuse your body and lead to sugar spikes.

🥣 Simple Rules to Follow:

- 🍽 **Late dinners = higher blood sugar overnight**
- 🕐 **Fixed meal times = better insulin response**
- ⏳ **Gaps between meals = pancreas gets time to rest**

⏱ Ideal Meal Timings for Sugar Control

Meal	Best Time	Tip
Breakfast	Within 1 hour of waking (7-9 AM)	Kickstart your metabolism
Lunch	12-2 PM	Make this your heaviest meal
Dinner	Before 7 PM	Light and early, 3 hours before sleep
Fasting	12-14 hours overnight	Helps body burn fat and reset insulin

✋Portion Control: Use Your Hand as a Guide

No calorie counting needed. Just use your hand!

Food Type	Portion Size	Examples
Protein	Palm size	Chicken, tofu, paneer, lentils
Carbs	Fist size	Brown rice, millet, fruits, veggies
Fats	Thumb size	Ghee, nuts, seeds, olive oil
Veggies	Two handfuls	Salads, cooked veggies

× *Common Mistakes People Make*

- 🍛 **Big dinners with little protein** – heavy night meals spike sugar.
- ☕ **Skipping or delaying breakfast** – leads to cravings and overeating later.
- 🍪 **All-day snacking** – keeps insulin high, stopping fat burn.

The No-Snacking Rule

Every time you eat, insulin is released. **More snacks = more insulin spikes.**
Instead:

- Stick to 3 proper meals.
- If hungry, drink water, herbal tea, or coconut water.
- Eat enough protein and fiber to stay full longer.

👦 📋 Real People, Real Results

💻 Amit – IT Professional

Used to skip breakfast and eat late dinners.
✓ Changed his meal timings and stopped snacking.
📊 Fasting sugar dropped from **160 → 115 mg/dL** in 6 weeks.

Rohit – Busy CEO

Ate airport food and late-night meals.
✓ Pre-planned meals and added early protein dinners.
📊 HbA1c dropped from **7.8% → 6.2%** in 8 weeks.

🗄 Manoj – Businessman

Ate irregularly and binged at night.
✓ Shifted to early lunch, light dinner, and home-cooked food.
📊 Post-meal sugar dropped from **240 → 140 mg/dL**, lost 6kg.

🏠 Sunita – Homemaker

Kept snacking while cooking. Ate leftovers late.
   ✔ Practiced mindful eating with set mealtimes.
   📊 Lost 5 kg and fasting sugar reduced by **30 mg/dL** in 6 weeks.

✔ Your Smart Eating Checklist

- ⏰ Eat meals at the **same time** every day.
- 🌙 Finish dinner **3 hours before bedtime**.
- ✋ Use your hand to guide **portion size**.
- Avoid frequent snacks—**give insulin a break**.
- 💧 Stay hydrated—**sometimes we eat when we're just thirsty**

💡 Final Thought:

You don't need fancy diets or calorie apps. Just **eat on time, eat smart**, and **let your body rest between meals**. Try this for **just one week**, and you'll feel the difference—more energy, better sugar control, and a lighter you!

Smart Eating

MEAL TIMING & PORTION CONTROL

Why when you eat matters as much as what you eat

BEST MEAL TIMES FOR SUGAR CONTROL	PORTION CONTROL: USE YOUR HAND!

 **BREAKFAST** 7-9 AM

 **LUNCH** 12-2 PM

 **DINNER** BEFORE 7PM

 **FASTING** 12-14 HRS

 **PROTEIN** (size of palm) chicken, paneer

 **CARBS** (fist) millets, fruit

 **FATS** (thumb) ghee, nuts

 **VEGGIES** (two handfuls) salads, cooked

COMMON MISTAKES PEOPLE MAKE

✗ BIG DINNERS LATE
✗ SKIPPING BREAKFAST
✗ ALL-DAY SNACKING

EAT ON TIME, EAT SMART!

15

The Hidden Truth Behind 'Healthy' Labels – Outsmarting the Food Industry

You walk into a supermarket, ready to buy something healthy. You see words like:

- "Sugar-Free"
- "Diabetes-Friendly"
- "No Added Sugar"

Sounds perfect, right?

Wrong. These are **marketing traps**—clever words designed to fool you. Behind the fancy labels may be ingredients that actually **raise your sugar levels**. But don't worry—this chapter will show you how to see through the lies and make truly **diabetes-friendly** choices.

✔ Step 1: Don't Trust the Front Label

The front of any package is there to **sell**, not to tell the truth.

Words like "Natural," "Healthy," or "Low-GI" (glycemic index) may sound good—but they don't always mean the product is safe for you.

✒ **Always flip the pack** and look at the **back label**.

✔ Step 2: Learn to Read the Nutrition Label

Here's what to look for:

1. Serving Size

- Many products show "low" carbs—but only for a tiny serving.
- Always check how many servings are in one pack.

2. Total Carbs vs. Net Carbs

☞ Use this simple formula:

Net Carbs = Total Carbs - Fiber - Sugar Alcohols

Why? Because fiber and some sugar alcohols (like erythritol) don't spike sugar.

🥷 *Example:*

- Total Carbs = 20g
- Fiber = 8g
- Erythritol = 5g
- ➡ **Net Carbs = 7g**

That's the number that affects your blood sugar.

3. Sugar Content

- More than 5g of sugar per serving? Not good.
- Even 1-2g matters if it's **added sugar**.

✔ Step 3: Watch for Hidden Sugars

Sugar has many names. Look out for:

- Fructose, Glucose, Dextrose
- High-Fructose Corn Syrup
- Agave Nectar, Coconut Sugar, Honey
- Date Syrup, Maltodextrin
- **Sugar Alcohols** like **Maltitol** or **Sorbitol** (yes—they can raise sugar too)

✔ Step 4: Check for "Added Sugars"

These are extra sugars **added during processing**—and they're the real problem.
   Why they're bad:

- They cause sugar spikes
- Increase fat storage
- Promote insulin resistance

 Hidden in things like sauces, cereals, flavored yogurt—even health drinks.
   🖋 Tip: Choose foods with **ZERO added sugar** on the label.

☑ Step 5: Don't Be Fooled by Fancy Words

Here's the truth behind common "healthy" claims:

Claim	Reality
"Sugar-Free"	Often full of artificial sweeteners or sugar alcohols
"No Added Sugar"	Can still contain high natural sugar from fruit concentrates
"Diabetes-Friendly"	No medical proof-just clever marketing
"Low Glycemic"	May still spike your sugar due to poor ingredient quality

☑ Step 6: Are Artificial Sweeteners Safe?

Some are okay, others are risky.

Sweetener	Safe or Not?	Reason
Stevia	✓ Safe	Natural, no sugar spike
Monk Fruit	✓ Safe	Natural, no sugar spike
Erythritol	✓ Safe	Minimal effect on sugar
Sucralose	✗ Risky	Can disturb gut health
Aspartame	✗ Risky	Linked to headaches, gut issues
Maltitol/Sorbitol	✗ Risky	Can raise sugar and cause bloating

✓ Step 7: Smart Grocery Shopping Tips

Follow these simple rules:

- Stick to **whole foods** – fruits, vegetables, nuts, seeds
- Choose foods with **short ingredient lists**
- If you **can't pronounce it**, don't buy it
- Always **compare brands** – even "healthy" yogurt can hide

more sugar than a dessert

🔍 Real-Life Shocker:

Many "sugar-free" cookies contain **more carbs than regular ones!** Why? Because of **starch, flour, and hidden sugars**.

✓ Quick Summary – Your Label Reading Checklist

✓ Flip the pack
  ✓ Check serving size
  ✓ Focus on **Net Carbs**, not just total carbs
  ✓ Watch for **added sugars** and fake sweeteners
  ✓ Look out for sugar's hidden names
  ✓ Choose products with real, whole ingredients

Challenge: Check 5 products in your kitchen

Pick any 5 items you already have at home and:

- Read the back label
- Look for hidden sugars
- Check the net carbs

You'll be shocked at what you find!

SUGAR-FREE?
LABEL READING CHEAT SHEET

READ THE BACK
Marketing lies on front! →

CHECK SERVING SIZE

Nutrition Facts
Serving size

SMALL SERVINGS HIDE CARBS!

$20g - 8g - 4g = 8g$

AVOID ADDED SUGAR

✓ **HIDDEN NAMES**

COUNT NET CARB

✓ Glucose
Corn syrup
Datee

⚠

CHOOSE WHOLE INGREDIENTS

IGNORE CLAIMS

• "NO SUGAR ADDED"

• "Natural"–
"Diabetes-Friendly"

FEWER IS BETTER!

CHOOSE WHOLE INGREDIENTS

16

Know Yourself Before You Heal Yourself

Before we talk about changing what you eat, how you move, or what time you sleep—it's important to understand where you are *right now*. Reversing diabetes starts with self-awareness. You can't change what you don't track.

Imagine This:

Trying to reverse diabetes without evaluating yourself is like trying to reach a destination without a map. You might take random turns, waste time, or get lost. But if you know where you are today, you can plan exactly how to move forward—and measure how far you've come.

🔍 Step 1: Understand Your Current Health (Your Baseline)

Get a clear picture of your internal health with these essential blood tests:

Marker	Ideal Range	Why It Matters
Fasting Blood Sugar (FBS)	70–90 mg/dL	Reflects your overnight sugar control
Post-Meal Sugar (PPBS)	< 140 mg/dL (2 hrs after meal)	Indicates how your body handles food
HbA1c	< 5.7%	Long-term blood sugar tracker (3 months avg.)
Fasting Insulin	< 8 mIU/L	Tells how hard your body is working to regulate sugar
Triglycerides	< 150 mg/dL	High levels signal insulin resistance
HDL (Good Cholesterol)	> 40 mg/dL (men)/ > 50 mg/dL (women)	Protects your heart and supports metabolism
Body Fat %	Varies by gender & age	Better indicator than weight or BMI

🧑 Step 2: Self-Check – How's Your Metabolism Doing?

Answer these questions honestly:

- Do you feel tired after meals?
- 🍭 Do you crave sweets often?
- Are you gaining weight even with "healthy" food?
- Do you urinate often or feel constantly thirsty?
- Do you struggle with brain fog or mood swings?

If you said YES to two or more—your metabolism is waving a red flag. But the good news is—you can fix it.

◻ Step 3: Keep a 7-Day Health Journal

Track these every day for the next week:

- 🥗 **All meals & snacks**
- ⚡ **Energy levels** after eating
- 🏃 **Physical activity** (even walking counts)
- **Sleep quality & hours**
- **Stress levels** during the day

Why? You'll discover patterns you never noticed before.

⚠ Step 4: Watch Out for Hidden Triggers

Some daily habits silently harm your health:

- ✘ Sugar-free or "healthy" packaged foods
- ✘ Granola bars, juices, flavored yogurts
- ✘ Late-night meals or frequent snacking
- ✘ Poor sleep (even 1 bad night increases sugar!)
- ✘ Skipping meals or eating too fast

🧑 Step 5: Set the Right Mindset

- ✓ *Reversal is 100% possible* (real people have done it!)
- ✓ *Your body wants to heal*—you just need to support it.
- ✓ *No quick fixes*—consistency beats perfection.
- ✓ *You're the CEO of your health*—take charge today.

Bonus: Go Deeper with CGM (Continuous Glucose Monitor)

Want to know how food affects you *in real time*? A CGM is a game changer.

📱 How CGM Works:

- Attach a small sensor to your arm.
- It reads your blood sugar 24/7.
- You get real-time data on a mobile app.

✅ Week 1: Observe (No changes yet—just eat normally)

✅ Week 2: Adjust (Now test changes in food, movement, sleep)

Why It Helps:

- Identify which foods spike your sugar
- Learn how stress, sleep, and walks affect you
- Get instant feedback on choices (no guesswork!)

Even 14 days with CGM can change your awareness—and your life.

* Action Plan: Your First Reversal Steps

Task	✅ Done?
Get your blood tests done	☐
Start your 7-day journal	☐
Identify sugar-spiking habits	☐
Set your mindset to win	☐
Try CGM for 14 days (if possible)	☐

💬 Final Thought:

You can't reverse what you don't measure. Start by understanding your body, your habits, and your mindset. This chapter is not about judgment—it's about clarity. Once you know your current status, you can move forward with confidence.

Your journey has officially begun. Let's keep going—together. 💪

KNOW YOURSELF BEFORE YOU HEAL YOURSELF

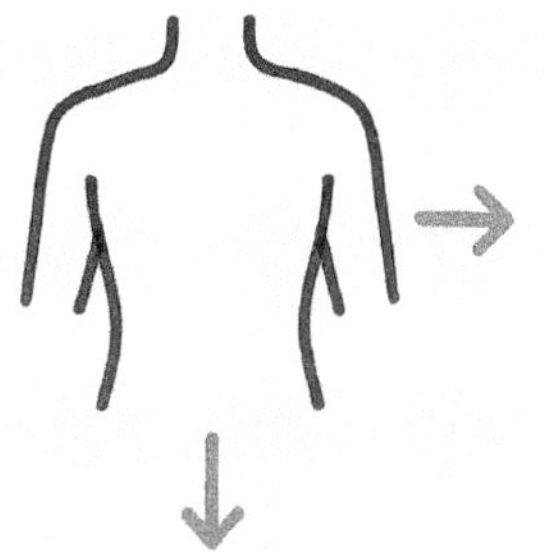

Get Blood Work Done

- Fasting Blood Sugar 70-90
- HbA1c Under 5.7%
- Fasting Insulin Lower 8
- Triglycerides
- Body Fat %

Get Blood Work Done

- Fasting Blood Sugar
- HbA1c Under 5.7%
- Fasting Insulin lower 8
- Are you often tired?

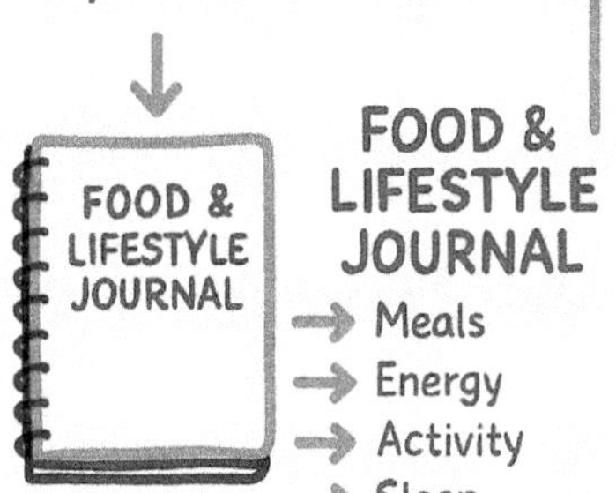

FOOD & LIFESTYLE JOURNAL

→ Meals
→ Energy
→ Activity
→ Sleep

Identify Triggers

- Hidden sugars
- Poor sleep
- Unhealthy snacks
- Sedentary lifestyle

Commit to the process with the right mindset

17

Continuous Glucose Monitoring (CGM): Your 24/7 Blood Sugar Guide

Imagine if your body could talk and tell you **exactly** what's going on inside—every time you eat, sleep, walk, or stress. That's what **Continuous Glucose Monitoring (CGM)** offers: a real-time window into how your blood sugar responds to your daily life. It's not just a gadget—it's your **personal health coach**, giving you data to make smarter choices and fast-track your diabetes reversal journey.

1. Why CGM Is a Game-Changer for Reversal

Traditional finger-prick tests give you just a moment in time. But **CGM tracks your blood sugar 24/7**, showing how it changes in response to:

- ✓ What you eat
- ✓ How you move
- ✓ How you sleep
- ✓ How stressed you are

No more guesswork. You'll see patterns, spot triggers, and learn which habits are helping—or hurting—you.

2. What to Watch for in Your CGM Readings

Understanding your CGM data is the key to unlocking reversal. Here's what to track:

📊 **Fasting Glucose**: Target below **100 mg/dL**

🍽 **After-Meal Spikes**: Aim for less than **30 mg/dL rise** post-meal

🌙 **Night Glucose Trends**: Watch for late-night rises (caused by stress, food, or poor sleep)

📈 **Glucose Stability**: A steady graph = better insulin sensitivity

> 💡 ***Goal:*** *Stable, smooth sugar levels—not spikes and crashes.*

3. Mistakes People Make (and How to Avoid Them)

Even with the best tech, some people miss the mark. Here's how to avoid common CGM pitfalls:

✖ Focusing too much on a single high reading

✔ Look at trends over days—not just one spike

✖ Ignoring meal composition

✔ Combine carbs with protein, fiber, and healthy fats

✖ Blaming only food

✔ Stress, poor sleep, and dehydration spike sugar too

✖ Collecting data but not acting on it

✔ Use insights to adjust meals, activity, and routines

4. How to Use CGM Effectively: A Step-by-Step Guide

◈ Step 1: Choose Your Device
Top picks include **Freestyle Libre**, **Dexcom**, or **Medtronic Guardian**—choose based on comfort, cost, and ease.

◈ Step 2: Apply the Sensor
A tiny patch (usually on the arm) monitors glucose from under the skin—**pain-free**, and most last **10–14 days**.

◈ Step 3: Track What You Do
Log meals, workouts, sleep, and stress. Use apps (like Libre-Link or Dexcom G6) to match actions with sugar trends.

◈ Step 4: Optimize Your Lifestyle Based on Data
📊 If rice spikes your sugar → switch to millets
🏃 If a 10-min walk lowers sugar → make it routine
If late dinners raise glucose → eat earlier

◈ Step 5: Review Every 2 Weeks
Ask:
🔍 Are fasting sugars improving?
🔍 Are post-meal spikes smaller?
🔍 Are my readings more stable overall?

Final Thought: CGM = Knowledge + Action

🗝 **CGM is your accountability partner.** It shows what works—and what doesn't.
🗝 **Use it to make data-driven changes.** With each insight, your reversal gets stronger.

📌 **Don't chase perfection—chase patterns.** Progress is the goal, not perfection.

> 💬 *"I used to think I was eating healthy… until my CGM showed sugar spikes after my so-called 'diabetes-friendly' snack bar."*

Your 14-Day CGM Challenge:

Try one CGM cycle (14 days). For the first 7 days, just observe. The next 7, adjust based on what you learned. Track results—you'll be amazed.

18

Know Your Starting Line: The DIY Metabolic Checkup

Before you start reversing diabetes, you need one thing above all: **clarity.**

Clarity about where you stand. Clarity about what's working (and what's not).

This chapter is your personal checkpoint—**a self-guided reality check**—so you can move forward with purpose, not guesswork.

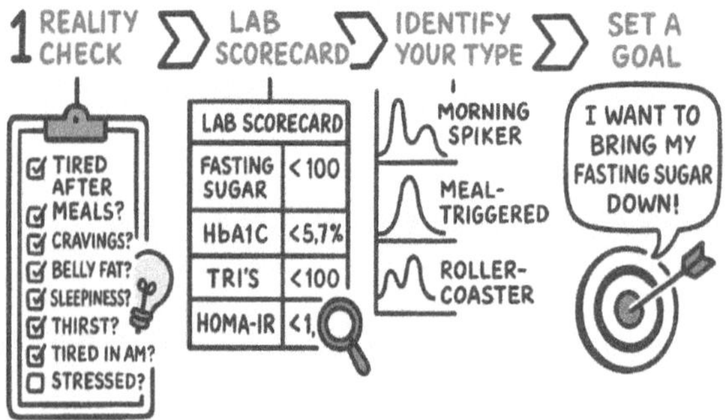

Question	Yes/No
Do you feel tired or low-energy after meals?	☐
Do you get frequent cravings, especially for sweets or carbs?	☐
Have you gained weight around the belly without major dietary changes?	☐
Do you feel sleepy or foggy after eating?	☐
Are you often thirsty or do you urinate frequently?	☐
Do you wake up tired even after a full night's sleep?	☐
Do you feel anxious, overwhelmed, or constantly stressed?	☐
Do you lack a consistent movement or exercise routine?	☐

💡 ***If you checked 'Yes' for 3 or more**, your body is likely struggling with **insulin resistance**—the core issue behind type 2 diabetes.*

🔬 Step 2: Your Lab Scorecard - What Do the Numbers Say?

Along with self-awareness, you need biomarkers to set your baseline and track improvement. Here's what to test:

Test	Ideal Range	Why It Matters
Fasting Blood Sugar	< 100 mg/dL	Checks liver glucose output
Post-Meal Sugar (1hr)	< 140 mg/dL	Measures carb processing ability
HbA1c (3-month average)	< 5.7%	Indicates long-term sugar control
Fasting Insulin	< 10 µU/mL	Measures insulin load in bloodstream
Triglycerides	< 100 mg/dL	Reflects fat metabolism efficiency
HOMA-IR	< 1.5	Reveals level of insulin resistance

> 🔖 **If your HOMA-IR is high**, it means your cells aren't responding well to insulin—your #1 target for reversal.

🔍 Step 3: Identify Your Glucose Type

Thanks to CGM (from the previous chapter), you can now **map your sugar pattern**. Most people fall into one of these:

The Morning High-Spiker
Wakes up with high sugar due to overnight glucose release.

The Meal-Triggered Spiker
Experiences sugar spikes after eating—often due to carb sensitivity.

The All-Day Rollercoaster
Wild sugar swings caused by stress, bad sleep, or irregular eating.

> 💡 Recognizing your **glucose pattern** helps you focus your efforts where it matters most.

◉ Step 4: Set Your Personal Reversal Goal

It's time to turn your insights into a target. Use this format:

"I want to bring my [fasting sugar / post-meal spike / HbA1c] from ____ to ____ in the next 3 months by making changes in [food / movement / sleep / stress]."

✓ **Examples**:

"I want to bring my **fasting sugar from 120 to 90 mg/dL** by walking after dinner and eating earlier."

"I want to bring my **HbA1c from 7.2% to under 6%** by switching from wheat to millet and managing stress better."

⟳ Your DIY Reversal Check-In Plan

Action	Why It Matters
✅ Track energy, cravings, mood, and sleep for 7 days	Builds awareness
✅ Get updated lab tests	Sets your baseline
✅ Use a CGM (if available)	Reveals real-time sugar patterns
✅ Reflect on your pattern & pick one priority goal	Keeps things actionable

💡 Final Thought: You Can't Fix What You Don't Measure

Reversal starts with awareness. When you truly **know your body**, every decision becomes easier.

You don't need to change everything overnight—just **start with clarity** and let progress build momentum.

Ready to take action based on your data? The next chapter will show you how to turn CGM insights
into smart, daily decisions that transform your sugar control.

19

Glucose in Action – Your Lifestyle Optimization Blueprint

You've explored your CGM patterns, assessed your health, and learned where your sugar spikes come from. Now it's time to take *real-time action*—not guesswork, but data-backed tweaks that move you closer to diabetes reversal.

Think of your CGM as your **personal lifestyle GPS**—it tells you when to reroute and when to stay the course. This chapter will help you analyze your data, make precise adjustments, and fine-tune your lifestyle week by week.

✓ Step 1: Identify What's Spiking Your Glucose

Your CGM gives you 24/7 insights—but how do you use them?
🔍 Look for these clues:

- **Post-meal spikes >30 mg/dL** or above **140 mg/dL** = Meal needs modification.
- **High fasting glucose** = Possible late-night meals, poor

sleep, or elevated cortisol.

- **Random spikes without food** = Could be from stress, dehydration, or intense workouts.
- **Flatline or dips** after meals = Possible overcompensation, under-eating, or insulin overreaction.

🎤 **CGM Insight**: It's not about hitting perfect numbers—it's about **stable trends**.

Step 2: Make Targeted Mini-Tweaks

No need to overhaul your life—just fix what the data highlights:

◈ **If Fasting Glucose is High:**

- Stop eating 3 hours before sleep
- Hydrate more and sleep earlier
- Add light evening activity like stretching or walking

◈ **If Post-Meal Glucose Spikes:**

- Shrink your carb portion
- Add **fiber + protein + fat** to slow absorption
- Walk for **10–15 mins** after meals

◈ **If Stress Causes Spikes:**

- Try **4-7-8 breathing** or mindfulness daily
- Add magnesium-rich foods (pumpkin seeds, spinach)
- Prioritize relaxation at least **once daily**

◈ **If Workouts Spike Sugar:**

- Try gentler sessions (yoga, walking) instead of HIIT
- Add a protein snack post-exercise
- Stay hydrated before & after workouts

🖊 **Micro-Tweaks Matter**: Small changes based on real data give you big wins without burnout.

🖼 Step 3: Weekly Self-Check Routine

Use a Sunday reflection ritual to stay on track:

1. What meals kept sugar stable?
2. What foods or habits spiked it?
3. Did post-meal walks help?
4. Was my sleep affecting morning sugar?

⚡ Make **1 or 2 changes** each week. Don't aim for perfection—aim for **progress**.

⚠ Common Pitfalls to Avoid

✕ **Freaking out over one spike**
→ Focus on *patterns*, not one-off numbers
✕ **Trying to fix everything at once**
→ You won't know what worked. Change one thing at a time.
✕ **Ignoring sleep and stress**
→ These two have a MASSIVE impact on insulin sensitivity.
✕ **Collecting data without acting**
→ Knowledge is power—only when used!

Final Word: CGM = Clarity + Control

Your CGM isn't a critic. It's your coach. It shows how YOUR body reacts—not what some app or influencer says should work. Use it to:

- Personalize your meal plan
- Choose optimal workout times
- Learn what habits sabotage or support you
- Build a lifestyle that heals your metabolism

The CGM gives you a **custom map**—all you need to do is follow the signals.

Next Up: Smart Meal Planning – Let's use your CGM data to build meals that work for *you*, not against you.

20

The Insulin Upgrade: Boost Sensitivity, Reverse Faster

You've already built your personalized meal plan using CGM insights. But here's the truth—if your body isn't responding well to insulin, even the cleanest diet won't take you far.

The real driver behind diabetes reversal? **Insulin Sensitivity**—the ability of your cells to respond to insulin efficiently.

This chapter will show you how to **train your body to use insulin better**, reduce resistance naturally, and fast-track your reversal journey.

What is Insulin Sensitivity, and Why Should You Care?

Insulin acts like a **key**, unlocking cells to absorb glucose from your blood. When your cells become "resistant," this key stops working properly.

   ✕ High blood sugar—even after healthy meals
   ✕ More insulin release = More fat storage + inflammation

✕ Energy crashes, cravings, and blocked fat burning

Reversal isn't about pumping more insulin—it's about making your body listen to it again.

The 4 Foundations of Insulin Sensitivity

1. Movement – Your Built-in Insulin Booster

Muscles are like glucose magnets. When you move, they soak up sugar—**even without insulin**.

✓ **Post-meal walks (10–15 min)** → Reduces glucose spikes by up to 50%

✓ **Strength training (2–3 times/week)** → Adds insulin receptors in muscle cells

✓ **NEAT (Non-Exercise Activity Thermogenesis)** → Standing, walking, fidgeting—all count!

💡 *Even 2 minutes of movement after meals can dramatically improve sugar response.*

2. Nutrition – Eat to Heal Insulin Resistance

Some foods **supercharge** insulin sensitivity. Others sabotage it.

Top Foods to Include

- Fermented foods (curd, idli, kanji, buttermilk)
- Magnesium-rich foods (spinach, almonds, pumpkin seeds)
- Cinnamon (½ tsp daily) – lowers fasting glucose

- Omega-3s (flaxseeds, chia seeds, fish)

🔘 Foods to Avoid

- Refined carbs (sugar, white bread, bakery snacks)
- Refined oils (sunflower, soybean)
- Artificial sweeteners (aspartame, sucralose)
- Reheated oils (causes inflammation)

🥢 *Food isn't just fuel—it's medicine. Choose it wisely.*

3. Stress + Sleep – The Silent Disruptors

Just one night of poor sleep can trigger insulin resistance the next day.

✔ 7–9 hours of restful sleep = Better glucose metabolism
✔ Digital detox before bed (no screens after 9 PM)
✔ Practice 4-7-8 or box breathing daily
✔ Magnesium supplementation (if needed)
💡 *Sleep is not a luxury—it's your body's healing zone.*

4. Fasting – Reset Your Insulin Clock

Fasting doesn't mean skipping meals—it means **giving your body time to rest** from insulin spikes.

🕐 Best Types for Beginners & Intermediates

- **12:12** (eat for 12 hours, fast for 12)

- **16:8** (eat in an 8-hour window)
- **Early Time-Restricted Eating (ETRE)**: Finish dinner by 6–7 PM

📌 *Fasting gives insulin a break, helping it reset and work better when you eat.*

📋 The Insulin Sensitivity Action Plan

Step 1 – Move daily (5K–10K steps) + 10-min walks after each meal

🥗 **Step 2** – Eat insulin-smart: fermented foods, magnesium-rich, low-GI meals

Step 3 – Fix your sleep, reduce stress using breathwork & light exposure control

⏱ **Step 4** – Try a 12-hour fast for 5 days a week and monitor how you feel

🏆 Why This Matters: Real Results Come From Sensitivity

◈ Boosting insulin sensitivity = **Less insulin needed** → **Less fat gain** → **Faster reversal**

◈ You don't need extreme diets—just smarter food and movement decisions

◈ Your body is not broken—it just needs a reset

🗂 How We Do It at Sixth Gear

At **Sixth Gear**, we go beyond advice. We help people like you integrate these strategies into real life:

✔ **Post-meal movement routines** personalized by CGM trends

✔ **Insulin-smart meal planning** using food pairing & timing

✔ **Fasting support plans** tailored to your lifestyle

✔ **Sleep & stress protocols** to supercharge your metabolic healing

We don't chase sugar numbers—we **restore full metabolic balance.**

Next Up → Smart Food Choices: Oils, Fruits, Fiber & Dairy that Heal Insulin Resistance

21

The Meal Order That Heals: Sixth Gear's Proven Sequencing Formula

At **Sixth Gear**, we believe **how you eat is just as important as *what* you eat**. Over time, we've refined a **meal sequencing method** that has helped many patients reduce their **HbA1c by up to 2.5%**, simply by changing the order in which they eat their food.

Many diabetics switch to 2 meals a day, thinking it will control sugar, but this often backfires. Long gaps between meals can trigger cortisol release, leading to insulin resistance and glucose spikes. Skipping breakfast especially worsens morning sugar levels. Without proper nutrient balance, this approach can cause fatigue, cravings, and weight gain. The key is not fewer meals— but smarter, well-timed ones.

This approach is simple, sustainable, and science-backed—and it delivers results.

✔ Why It Works:

- Keeps blood sugar levels steady throughout the day
- Enhances insulin sensitivity
- Improves digestion and helps you feel full longer

➾ The Sixth Gear Meal Sequencing Formula

1. Begin with a Protein-Rich Breakfast

Why: Protein in the morning sets the tone for the day. It prevents energy crashes, controls cravings, and avoids the glucose spike from carb-heavy breakfasts.

What to Eat:

- ◯ Eggs, paneer, tofu, sprouts
- ⊛ Moong dal or besan chilla
- ⛾ Unsweetened protein smoothie
- ◉ Hand-pounded millet dosa

🖋 **Avoid:** Poha, bread, idli, cornflakes—these cause early blood sugar spikes and leave you hungry sooner.

2. Main Meals (Lunch & Dinner) – Eat in This Sequence

✓ Step 1: Start with Fiber (Raw Salad & Vegetables)
Why: Fiber slows down glucose absorption and preps your digestive system.
Options:

- 🥗 Cucumber, carrots, radish, bell peppers
- 🌿 Raw sprouts with lemon and salt
- 🥦 Lightly steamed greens (broccoli, spinach, cabbage)

✓ Step 2: Add Protein (Lentils, Eggs, Paneer, Tofu)
Why: Protein supports insulin release without causing a sugar spike.
Options:

- 🍳 Boiled eggs, paneer, tofu
- 🍲 Chana dal, moong dal, masoor dal

✓ Step 3: Eat Cooked Vegetables
Why: Cooked veggies offer minerals and aid digestion.
Options:

- Methi, ridge gourd, pumpkin, bitter melon
- 🥘 Stir-fried mixed vegetables with spices

✓ Step 4: End with One Carb Source Only
Why: Limiting carbs to one type per meal reduces the glycemic load.
Choose ONE:

- 🍞 1 Roti (preferably jowar, bajra, or foxtail millet)
- 🍚 ½ cup hand-pounded or brown rice

📌 **Avoid combining** roti and rice or eating large portions—this can cause immediate spikes in blood sugar.

🔬 Why This Formula Works - Backed by Science

Step	Benefit
Fiber First	Slows sugar absorption, preps digestion
Protein Next	Boosts satiety, reduces insulin load
Veggies	Provides micronutrients for metabolic balance
Carbs Last & Limited	Prevents sugar overload

📊 Studies show this sequencing method can **cut post-meal glucose spikes by 50% or more.**

📊 Real Results from Sixth Gear Clients

- Average HbA1c reduction: **1.8% to 2.5%**
- ✔ Eliminated post-meal crashes
- ✔ Controlled hunger & reduced cravings
- ✔ Better energy, sleep, and mood stability

💡 Final Thought:

This method is **not a diet—it's a rhythm.**
Eat in the right order. Stay consistent. Watch your sugar stabilize without extreme restrictions.

22

Sweet Trap: The Bitter Truth About Artificial Sweeteners

In the race to reduce sugar, many people with diabetes turn to artificial sweeteners, believing they're a smarter, safer choice. After all, they promise sweetness without calories or sugar spikes—what's not to love?

But behind those shiny "sugar-free" and "diabetes-friendly" labels lies a bitter truth: artificial sweeteners may be silently sabotaging your reversal journey.

⊚ What Exactly Are Artificial Sweeteners?

Artificial sweeteners are lab-made compounds that taste hundreds of times sweeter than sugar. They're used in everything from "diet" sodas to sugar-free chocolates, cookies, protein bars, and even toothpaste and medications.

Common artificial sweeteners include:

- **Aspartame** (Equal, NutraSweet)
- **Sucralose** (Splenda)

- **Saccharin** (Sweet'N Low)
- **Acesulfame K** (Sunett)
- **Maltitol & Sorbitol** (Sugar alcohols used in many "low-carb" snacks)

They're marketed as safe and blood sugar–friendly. But let's uncover what really happens when you consume them regularly.

⚠ The Hidden Dangers of Artificial Sweeteners

1. They Confuse Your Body

Even though sweeteners have no calories, your brain and pancreas react to the sweetness anyway. This leads to:

- **Insulin spikes** even without real sugar
- **Fat storage** due to unused insulin
- **Cravings for carbs and sweets** as the body looks for the missing calories

☞ **Result:** You eat more, feel less satisfied, and can gain weight despite being "sugar-free."

2. They Damage Your Gut Microbiome

Your gut is home to trillions of bacteria that influence your metabolism and immune system. Artificial sweeteners:

- Kill off good bacteria
- Encourage bad microbes
- Lead to **insulin resistance and inflammation**

☞ **Result:** Your digestion, immunity, and blood sugar control get worse over time.

3. They Increase the Risk of Metabolic Syndrome

Studies show regular intake of artificial sweeteners is linked to:

- High blood pressure
- Abnormal cholesterol
- Elevated blood sugar
- Increased belly fat

☞ **Result:** You end up moving **closer to diabetes complications**, not away from them.

✔ Smarter Swaps: Natural Sweeteners That Support Reversal

Not all sweeteners are equal. Here are **safe, natural alternatives**:

🌿 Stevia

- Plant-based, zero calories
- No impact on blood sugar

🍈 Monk Fruit Extract

- 150–200 times sweeter than sugar
- Safe for blood sugar & gut

🍯 Raw Honey / Date Syrup (In moderation)

- Contains nutrients & antioxidants
- Use only in small quantities and with protein/fat to slow absorption

📌 **Pro Tip:** Train your taste buds to enjoy less sweetness over time—it's one of the most powerful changes you can make.

◉ Final Takeaway: Real Sweetness Comes from Real Health

Artificial sweeteners may help you cut calories, but they won't help you **reverse diabetes**. In fact, they might make it harder.

At **Sixth Gear**, we've seen true reversal happen not by swapping sugar with chemicals—but by **resetting the body through whole foods, fiber, healthy fats, and mindset shifts**.

If you truly want freedom from diabetes, start by breaking free from artificial fixes. Focus on nourishing your body with what's **real, natural, and healing**.

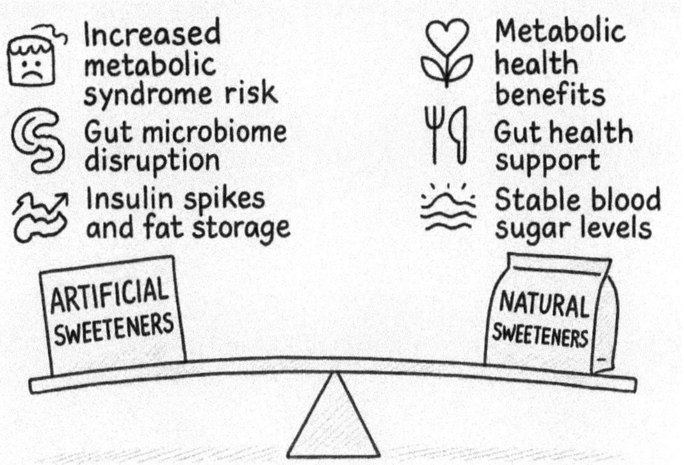

Increased metabolic syndrome risk
Gut microbiome disruption
Insulin spikes and fat storage
Metabolic health benefits
Gut health support
Stable blood sugar levels
ARTIFICIAL SWEETENERS
NATURAL SWEETENERS

23

Stress – The Silent Saboteur of Diabetes Reversal

When we talk about reversing diabetes, most people jump straight to food and exercise. But there's a powerful—and often ignored—enemy that can silently undo all your hard work: **stress**.

Chronic stress doesn't just affect your mood. It **disrupts hormones**, **raises blood sugar**, **triggers cravings**, and **worsens insulin resistance**. If you're serious about reversing diabetes, you must learn to master your stress.

💣 How Stress Triggers Insulin Resistance

1. The Cortisol Connection

Stress activates the body's survival mode. It releases **cortisol**, your primary stress hormone. While helpful in short bursts (like escaping danger), **chronic cortisol** wreaks havoc on your blood sugar.

Here's what it does:

115

- Raises blood sugar by signaling the liver to release more glucose
- Makes cells resistant to insulin
- ⬤ Promotes belly fat storage (which worsens insulin resistance)

☞ The result? Even with a healthy diet, your blood sugar may remain high if stress isn't managed.

2. Stress Fuels Emotional Eating

When stressed, we instinctively crave comfort foods—usually loaded with sugar, carbs, or fat. Why? Because they trigger a dopamine release, offering short-term emotional relief.

But here's the trap:

- ↑ Quick sugar spike
- ↓ Crash and fatigue
- ↻ More cravings → more spikes → more insulin resistance

☞ Emotional eating becomes a vicious cycle that silently sabotages your progress.

3. Stress = Poor Sleep = Poor Glucose Control

One of stress's sneakiest effects? **Ruining your sleep.**

Lack of restful sleep causes:

- Elevated cortisol the next day
- Increased hunger hormones (ghrelin)
- Reduced insulin sensitivity

☞ You wake up feeling tired and craving sugar—and the cycle repeats.

🧘 Your Anti-Stress Toolkit for Diabetes Reversal

Managing stress isn't just about feeling better—it's a metabolic strategy.

Here are **science-backed ways** to lower stress and improve blood sugar:

✔ Deep Breathing & Meditation

- Practice box breathing (Inhale 4s – Hold 4s – Exhale 4s – Hold 4s)
- Try mindfulness or guided meditation for 10 minutes daily

🩸 *Why it works:* Activates the parasympathetic (rest-and-digest) system, lowers cortisol, and improves insulin sensitivity.

✔ Movement as Medicine
- Go for a walk when stress hits
- Do yoga or gentle stretching
- Strength training 2–3 times/week

🩸 *Why it works:* Exercise boosts endorphins and regulates blood sugar.

✔ Prioritize Deep Sleep

- Maintain a consistent sleep-wake schedule
- Avoid screens at least 1 hour before bed
- Use herbal teas, magnesium, or relaxing music

🖉 *Why it works:* Deep sleep resets cortisol and enhances insulin function overnight.

✔ Nature Time

- Take a walk in the park
- Sit under a tree or do balcony gardening

🖉 *Why it works:* Studies show 20 minutes in nature reduces cortisol and improves blood pressure, mood, and metabolism.

✔ Talk It Out or Laugh It Off

- Call a friend, join a support group, or simply play with a pet or child
- Watch something funny—laughter really is the best medicine

🖉 *Why it works:* Human connection lowers stress hormones and boosts mood chemicals.

✔ Use Herbal Adaptogens (Ayurveda-Backed)

- **Ashwagandha** – Regulates cortisol, boosts energy
- **Brahmi** – Calms the mind, improves focus
- **Tulsi (Holy Basil)** – Balances mood and reduces oxidative stress

🔍 *Why it works:* Adaptogens support your adrenal glands and improve resilience to stress.

💡 Final Thought: You Can't Reverse Diabetes Without Reversing Stress

Stress is **invisible**—but its effects are very real.

At **Sixth Gear**, we help patients balance both their **external habits** and **internal chemistry**. And when stress is tamed, blood sugar often follows.
So remember:

- Your meals matter.
- Your movement matters.
- But your **mindset and stress levels** might matter most of all.

🌿 *Control stress, and you control your health.*

24

Hydration – The Hidden Hero of Diabetes Reversal

Most people track their meals, monitor sugar, and even exercise regularly—but completely overlook one of the simplest, most powerful tools for blood sugar control: **WATER**.

Yes, hydration isn't just good for glowing skin or digestion. It plays a **critical role** in how your body regulates insulin, breaks down fat, and maintains stable blood sugar levels.

💡 Why Water Matters More Than You Think

1. Water Helps Flush Out Excess Sugar

Your kidneys need water to eliminate excess glucose through urine. When you're dehydrated, this process slows down—and your blood sugar rises.

✓ More water = More glucose flushed out = Better control

2. Hydration = Better Insulin Sensitivity

When you're dehydrated, your body increases **vasopressin**, a hormone that tells your liver to release stored sugar into the blood. This leads to higher blood glucose—even if you haven't eaten anything.

✓ Staying hydrated keeps vasopressin levels low and insulin function smooth.

3. Boosts Metabolism & Cellular Energy
Water supports:

- Nutrient absorption
- Fat breakdown
- Mitochondrial function (your cell's energy engines)

☞ That means faster metabolism and improved insulin response—two critical pieces in reversing diabetes.

⬦ How to Hydrate for Maximum Blood Sugar Control

Here's your **Hydration Toolkit** for better glucose stability:

✔ Begin Your Day with Water

Drink 1 glass of warm or room-temp water upon waking to activate digestion and detox pathways.

✔ Water Before Meals

Drink a glass 30 minutes before meals—it aids digestion, prevents overeating, and curbs unnecessary cravings.

✔ Follow the 8x8 Rule

Aim for at least **8 glasses (2 liters)** daily. If you sweat more, talk a lot, or are very active, increase accordingly.

✔ Infuse It with Healing Herbs

Herbal waters are a win-win! They hydrate and support insulin function.

Great options:

- 🌿 **Cinnamon water** – Improves insulin sensitivity
- 🌿 **Ginger water** – Aids digestion & blood flow
- 🌿 **Tulsi water** – Reduces cortisol and blood sugar

✔ Watch Your Urine

💚 Light yellow = Hydrated
⚪ Dark yellow = Dehydrated (Time to drink up!)

✔ Limit These Glucose Saboteurs

- Sugary beverages
- Excess caffeine (especially black tea & coffee)
- Alcohol (dehydrates and affects liver glucose release)

🔏 These drinks spike blood sugar and **pull water out of your system**.

✔ Final Takeaway: Water Is More Than a Drink—It's a Metabolic Tool

Staying hydrated:

- Boosts insulin performance
- Reduces glucose spikes
- Supports energy and fat burn
- Makes every other diabetes-reversal habit more effective

You don't need fancy supplements—just fill up your glass!

☞ *So, are you drinking enough water today?*

Hydration Cycle for Diabetes Reversal

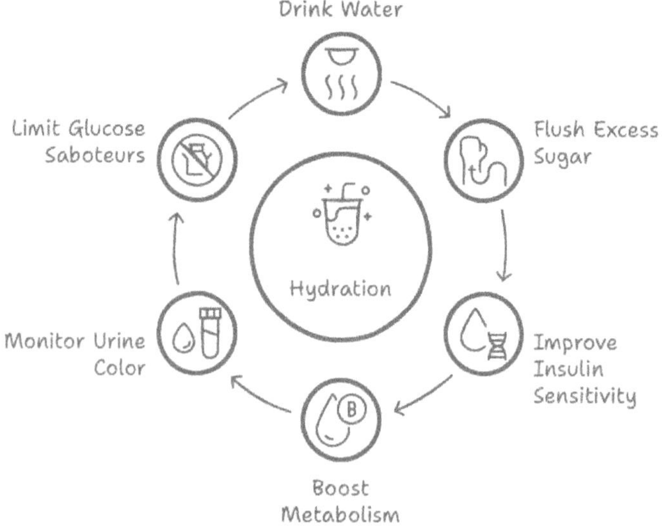

25

Herbal Remedies & Diabetes: Facts, Myths & Smart Choices

In a world full of "natural" promises and quick-fix solutions, herbal remedies have become a favorite buzzword—especially when it comes to diabetes. From Instagram influencers to ancient wisdom claims, the idea of reversing diabetes with herbs alone is both **tempting and confusing**.

Let's cut through the noise and uncover what really works, what's hyped, and how to use herbs **wisely and safely** on your path to reversal.

ᠬ Why Herbal Remedies Are So Popular

Herbs promise:

- "No side effects"
- "Time-tested results"
- "100% natural solutions"

And yes, traditional systems like Ayurveda, TCM (Traditional

Chinese Medicine), and naturopathy have long used herbs for managing blood sugar. Some of the most popular include:

- **Karela (Bitter Gourd)** – May reduce glucose levels
- **Methi (Fenugreek)** – Improves insulin sensitivity
- **Cinnamon** – Antioxidant and glucose-lowering effects
- **Gurmar (Gymnema Sylvestre)** – Known as the "sugar destroyer"
- **Amla (Indian Gooseberry)** – Rich in Vitamin C, supports pancreatic function
- **Jamun Seeds** – Used in powdered form to manage post-meal sugar
- **Vijaysar Wood** – Traditionally used to store water for subtle glucose-lowering benefits

But here's the big question...

! Do They Really Work?

✔ The Truth: Some Do, But With Limitations

- **Mild to Moderate Effects** – Herbs may help support blood sugar, but rarely reverse diabetes on their own.
- **Not a Substitute for Lifestyle Change** – Diet, movement, sleep, and stress matter much more.
- **Scientific Evidence Is Still Growing** – Most studies are small, and results vary widely.
- **No Dosage Standardization** – The same herb can have different effects depending on how it's grown or processed.

Beware of Marketing Gimmicks

Herbal supplement ads are often full of **half-truths** and **clever traps**:

🔍 Common Red Flags:

- "Clinically Proven!" (but no study or citation provided)
- "30-Day Reversal Formula" (unrealistic and unsafe)
- Glowing before-after photos (heavily edited or staged)
- Celebrity endorsements (paid promotions ≠ medical proof)
- Fear-based messaging ("Allopathy is poison!")

☞ **Reality check**: If something sounds too good to be true—it probably is.

👹 How to Make Safe, Smart Herbal Choices

If you choose to explore herbal options, do it right:

✔ Your Herbal Checklist

- **Research from scientific or clinical sources**
- **Consult your doctor or certified Ayurvedic expert** before mixing with medications
- **Look for safety certifications** (FSSAI, AYUSH, etc.)
- **Start small** and monitor your blood sugar regularly
- **Use herbs to complement**, not replace your lifestyle plan

🌿 Top Herbal Allies (When Used Smartly)

Herb	Potential Benefit	Use With Caution If...
Karela (Bitter Gourd)	Lowers blood glucose naturally	You're already on sugar-lowering meds
Methi (Fenugreek)	Increases insulin sensitivity	You have a sensitive stomach
Gurmar	Suppresses sweet cravings	You're hypoglycemic
Amla	Boosts immunity, lowers sugar	Taken in large doses with other acidic foods
Cinnamon	Reduces fasting blood sugar	Used in large quantities

☆ Final Word: Herbs Are Helpers, Not Heroes

Herbal remedies **can** support your diabetes reversal journey—but only when used with knowledge, care, and balance.

They won't replace:

- Smart meal planning
- Daily movement
- Stress and sleep management
- Your doctor's advice

But they **can** complement all of these beautifully—**if you use them wisely.**

🧘 Stay Rooted in Wisdom, Not Hype

Think of your diabetes journey like growing a tree. Herbs are like sunlight—supportive and nourishing—but without the **soil (lifestyle)** and **water (consistency)**, that tree won't grow.

💡 Be mindful. Be informed. And remember—**natural doesn't always mean safe, but informed always means empowered.**

A Message from My Heart to Yours

As we reach the final chapter of this journey together, I want to thank you—deeply and sincerely—for allowing me to walk beside you. The fact that you've made it this far tells me one thing: you're ready. Ready to reclaim your health, break free from the grip of diabetes, and step boldly into a life filled with energy, purpose, and joy.

To the many patients who have reversed their diabetes—you are my inspiration. Your courage, consistency, and belief have been the driving force behind this mission. And to those who paused or veered off the path—I want you to know that your journey still matters. You've taught me invaluable lessons about resilience, patience, and the power of trying again.

Let me remind you: **Diabetes is not your destiny.** It's a condition that can be reversed, managed, and understood—when you are equipped with the right knowledge and take daily, intentional steps.

This book was never meant to be just a collection of facts or advice—it was a **conversation**. A reflection of my lived experiences, my patients' victories, and my unwavering belief that you, too, have the strength to rewrite your story.

You are not walking this road alone. You are part of a growing community that chooses empowerment over helplessness and consistent action over fear.

As you move forward:

- Be kind to yourself.
- Celebrate every small win.
- Treat each challenge as a lesson, not a setback.
- And above all, keep remembering **why** you started.

If this book has sparked hope in you, shifted your perspective, or helped you take your first step—I consider my mission fulfilled.

I believe in you. I'm cheering for you. And I can't wait to hear your story of your victory. Here's to your vibrant, diabetes-free life. ❧ With unwavering support.

Dr. Mahesh D. Patil
Author · Mentor · Diabetes Reversal Coach